tarot

talks to the
woman within

teach yourself to rely on her support

cassandra eason

quantum

LONDON • NEW YORK • TORONTO • SYDNEY

quantum
An imprint of W. Foulsham & Co. Ltd
The Publishing House, Bennetts Close,
Cippenham, Slough, Berkshire, SL1 5AP, England

ISBN 0–572–02614-5

Printed in Great Britain by St. Edmundsbury Press, Bury St. Edmunds, Suffolk.

tarot

talks to the
woman within

Contents

Introduction

✛

The Tarot is the most visual of all the divinatory systems, like a brilliantly coloured picture book from childhood. For in a sense that is what it is, a psychic gallery of 78 images, referring to basic concepts and situations in life; each card is like a separate story book, or a door into a library of associated volumes, or a self-opening file on a computer, triggering a wealth of related symbols. What is more, because the pictures address the visual part of the brain, they are able to tap the same psychic abilities accessed by children, who have the ability to read minds or make accurate premonitions, a talent we lose when we move into adulthood. So Tarot divination is very good as an introductory psychic art or for the more experienced practitioner as a particularly evocative medium for intuitive and clairvoyant abilities. Tarot cards can be selected without conscious thought from a face-down, shuffled pack to offer guidance to a specific question or area of concern. The process is known as divination, whereby the *divus*, in earlier times regarded a deity, angel or spirit, influenced the selection to convey a message. In more modern terminology, it is the *divus within*, the Spiritual or Higher Power within each woman that guides our choices. Tarot cards can also be used as a focus for personal spiritual development, following the ancient art of scrying, focusing on a single card for associated thoughts, images and inspirations.

The Tarot pack

The Tarot pack is made up of 78 cards: 22 major cards, or Trumps as they were traditionally called, 40 numbered cards in four suits (similar to playing card suits but with different names) and 16 Court (royal personage) cards. The Tarot cards can be used to answer virtually any question, to choose between options or to plan a future path.

After shuffling the pack, a number of cards are chosen, face down, by the person asking the question (sometimes called the *Querant*) and then interpreted by the reader.

Basic spreads or layouts consist of three, six or nine cards that when read together build up a picture of the issue under question and suggest opportunities, strategies and ways of overcoming obstacles. There are many layouts, complex and simple, and later in this book I have suggested a few that can be used for different purposes. Examples include an Options Spread (see page 163) in which two separate rows of cards are chosen to explore the consequences of making different choices, and a Calendar Spread (see page 157), which assigns two cards for each month, to plan out the year ahead.

The Major Arcana

The Major Arcana is made up of 22 cards that can vary slightly in order and name, depending on the type of pack. The word *arcana* means 'hidden secrets' and this group of cards are sometimes used alone in readings, especially for matters concerning the inner world of the questioner, the self, rather than relationships. They are based on what Jung called the 'archetypes', the idealised forms of human states, the unopened book or what we might in computer terms call the zip file.

The Major Arcana cards have tales to tell, drawing on history and myth for the characters they portray. These include the Mother, the Father, the Divine Child, the Trickster (who is necessary to trigger change and self-awareness), the Virgin, the Hero, the Lovers (sometimes represented as the Sacred Marriage), the Holy Man (or Woman) and the Recluse. Here also you will find cosmic forces, the Sun, the Moon and the Stars and concepts and principles such as justice, moderation, endurance and the Willing Sacrifice.

In the actual Tarot pack, these characters have specific representations: the Mother appears as the Empress; the Father is the Emperor; the Divine Child is the Fool; the Trickster is the Magician; the Virgin is the High Priestess; the Hero is the charioteer in the Chariot card; the Holy Man or Woman is the Hierophant; the Recluse is the Hermit and the Willing Sacrifice is the Hanged Man. The Lovers appear as themselves.

Because these concepts and personalities span so many cultures and ages, the Tarot's origins have been identified in many traditions, and this is reflected in the bewildering variety of pack designs, which reflect the cultures of India, ancient Egypt, mediaeval Europe, the Romany gypsies and the Celts. The card names and the words we use to explain them are only part of the Tarot experience, and whether you are reading for yourself or others, the true understanding of the Tarot pack is already embedded in the consciousness of all of us, through the memories we have inherited via our ancestral genes from the pool of collective wisdom. Women find it especially easy to accept this hidden wisdom – men tend to probe about in the depths of the psyche, as though exploring a darkened room with a torch, demanding who is speaking to them and not realising that the voice they are hearing is an echo of the wise, timeless part of themselves.

Some women use only the Major Arcana cards in readings and they can be valuable indicators of life changes and our inner world and are especially valuable for core issues or questions of spiritual concern. The Major Arcana are also generally used for meditation, as focal points for magical rituals and for psychic development work or scrying.

The Minor Arcana

The Minor Arcana includes 40 cards numbered from ace (one) to ten in each of four suits that correspond with the four traditional playing-card suits: Diamonds, Hearts, Clubs and Spades. The Tarot suits are named Pentacles (coins or discs), Cups (chalices), Wands (spears or staves) and Swords, and they also represent what the ancients regarded as the basic elements of which life was composed: Earth, Water, Fire and Air. These elements, it was believed, combined to form a fifth element, *Akasha,* or Ether, the synthesis of the others. In Tarot divination, as in magic generally, it is believed that the psychic energy produced in elemental fusion creates a sacred space in which answers even to seemingly insoluble questions can be found. In a reading, Number Cards tend to refer to specific issues and courses of action and are generally used either as part of a full pack reading or in conjunction with the Court Cards.

The Court Cards

There are 16 Court Cards – four more than the usual playing-card deck. The Jack takes on two aspects, the Page and the Knight (sometimes the Page is regarded as a younger female and the Knight a younger man) though the actual titles may vary slightly from pack to pack. Court Cards, which refer to personalities or aspects of personalities, are excellent for exploring relationship issues, whether alone, or as part of the full pack, or with the Major or Minor Arcana alone.

The origins of Tarot

Tarot cards were a mediaeval creation, although the images and themes are much older. The earliest surviving Tarot cards are in the *Bibliothèque Nationale* in Paris, where there are 17 ornate cards, 16 of them Tarot trumps. Recent research suggests they are Italian, dating from about 1470.

This would support the theory that Tarot cards may have originated from the north of Italy, in the valley of the River Taro which is a tributary of the River Po, hence the Italian name *Tarrochi* and the French name *Tarot*.

Another theory claimed that the gypsies brought the Tarot with them in their long trek to Europe from India via the Middle East. Certainly, many of the great Romany families of the past had old and very beautiful sets. The Arabic word *tariqua* ('the way of wisdom') bears some resemblance to Tarot, and the ancient Egyptian word *ta-rosh* means 'the royal way'.

The greatest influence on modern Tarot reading was Arthur Edward Waite who in 1891 joined the Order of the Golden Dawn, a mystical group who studied ancient wisdom. The Rider Waite

Tarot pack, with its illustrated Minor Arcana, was regarded not only as a tool for divination, but also believed to encourage visionary insight through meditative and magical techniques. Waite was also the first to associate the four suits with the four sacred objects of the Holy Grail quest which, according to legend, were brought in 64 AD by Joseph of Arimethea to Glastonbury (see page 90 for details of these).

Many of Waite's cards reflect the romantic Arthurian background of the Grail legends and many modern sets of Tarot cards, even those without illustrated Minor Arcanas, use the Waite interpretations of meaning.

Reading the Tarot

Hermes Trisimegistus, the first-century semi-divine Egyptian sorcerer who was regarded as the father of Western magic, is credited with the creation of *The Emerald Tablet*, said to contain the core of all magic. It began with the words: 'As above, so below'. If, as this suggests, it is possible to tap into cosmic energies through divinatory processes, then a Tarot card reading can predict not a fixed future, but the prevailing energies and interconnectedness between our personal path and choices and the wider patterns of life and the universe.

The psychologist Gustav Carl Jung believed that our 'collective unconscious', accessed through unconscious processes, offered the experiences and accumulated wisdom of mankind that operate outside the confines of time and space. This level of experience enables us to move beyond the limited vision that reveals only present and past, to glimpse possibilities and choices just over the horizon. Some kind of mind–power, perhaps akin to psychokinesis, a scientifically demonstrated ability whereby the mind can move inanimate objects, influences our apparently random selection of cards. In this context, people think of Uri Geller and spoon-bending, but the power is also implicated in poltergeist activity, physical mediumship and above all divination, whereby the deeper levels of the unconscious mind guide the hand to select exactly the relevant card, crystal or rune (see also my books on runes and crystals, also in the series *Talk to the Woman Within*). As I have discovered in the thousands of readings I have carried out over the past ten years, this power does work every time and the cards that are turned over reveal potential opportunities and paths which, if followed, do bring fulfilment.

Women and the Tarot

Women are masters in the art of juggling different aspects of their lives. I am writing this chapter on Boxing Day, having cooked the lunch, mended broken presents, soothed teenage angst and boosted damaged egos for a family confined like rats in a tinsel-covered cage. Almost ten years ago, when I was writing my first Tarot book, I was a working mother with five young children and I discovered that for many women, magic and divination had to be slotted into spare moments during the day; but I knew that it was important not to be deterred by lack of time or to think that spiritual awareness could only be acquired by those who had the time to spare to meditate in beautiful places or study volumes of ancient wisdom.

During the ten years since my first book, women have made great advances in the workplace and the home. They now go into battle on active service at sea, work full-time or take time out to travel alone and realise that a ring on the finger and baby in the cot are not, as many of my own generation were taught to believe, the only ways to fulfilment – and certainly not the right ones for everyone. My own daughters are confident and independent and seem to be entirely free from the huge burden of guilt I inherited from my own relationship with my late mother.

But women do still have pressures, for while in the 1980s we were promised we could *have it all*, the media hype forgot to mention that meant *doing it all*. The wealth of opportunities we have nowadays may give an exciting, fulfilling life, but the resulting pressures bring in their wake exhaustion, with many women feeling too tired for sex and eating disorders rapidly increasing. What is more, with the average age of first-time mothers having risen to 30 and many women having babies in their mid-forties, the day a child leaves school may coincide with its mother's retirement – and yet we live in a world that worships youth.

What is more, life today with mobile phones, fax, e-mail, 24-hour TV channels, all-night shopping malls, artificial lighting and central heating have turned night into day, winter into summer. We have lost the sense of silence and solitude and the natural ebbs and flows that mirror a woman's inner tides, so that many women feel constantly stressed and unable to relax. Modern women follow a male solar lifestyle rather than their natural affinities with the Moon, which date back to palaeolithic times.

The Tarot with its evocative imagery and gentle rituals of divination or meditation, perhaps by candlelight or moonlight, with fragrant oils burning in the deep silence of a sleeping house or in the soft light of dawn, centres on women, young and old, and links them through the universal archetypes with all women in all places and ages, who yearned for something more. But, over the years, I have learned that it is all too easy to do as I have done too often, to lose sight of yourself and your unique worth. So it is important, no matter how busy your life may be, to create a special time, your Tarot time, to lay out your life in the cards and treasure the insights you gain. Tarot time is akin to opening up your dreams, all the layers of experience, ideas, ideals and unexplored potentials within you. As you follow day by day the unfolding of your unique Tarot story, contained in the cards you select, so your pathway becomes clearer as you learn to trust your own powers, not only in readings but in life.

The Tarot and you

The popular image of the Tarot reader is frequently one of a mysterious, aloof, elegant female in a dimly lit, opulent room, who speaks in hushed tones and, like a psychic headmistress, delivers your future, cut, dried and set in concrete boots. In a sense, that is an image created by our consumer society, which believes that the more expensive the clairvoyant is the better her advice will be – and the more favourable the prophecies she will deliver. It was not until the 1960s that Tarot cards became available outside the

Romany/occult market. Now they can be bought in department stores, even in a packaged set in supermarkets. But the mystique has remained, together with the misconception that real Tarot readers are different and do not travel on the 17.55 from Waterloo to Surbiton. But that is just hype – we all have psychic abilities, and with practice you can learn to read for yourself and others, not to offer platitudes or predictions, but to offer some understanding of the myriad possibilities that lie ahead of us all.

Learning the meanings and the card layouts, or spreads, is the easy part. The difficulty comes in letting go of our preconceived ideas: it is like suddenly striking out from the edge of a swimming pool or aiming for the centre of an ice rink. It is important to let go of what a card *should* mean and the way a spread *should* be interpreted. On occasions when I have been teaching the Tarot, often the very best readings were made by students who have known none of the conventional meanings, but let the pictures tell their own story. I myself give my very best readings late at night on an all-night radio show when I am tired and I do not try to analyse the cards but let my psyche or inner voice speak. If you are ever at a loss with a reading, use the cards to weave a story and the answers will become clear .

Finally, it is important to give yourself time for your Tarot, to set aside a special hour or so away from the hurly-burly of your daily routine, to concentrate on your readings and your inner thoughts. With this in mind, I have presented this book in days, rather than chapters, with each section providing enough new information for you to read at one session. Of course, in practice, the time you have available for yourself will vary, as will your level of enthusiasm – and energy! So do not feel constrained to follow my suggestions for your days slavishly; be guided by your needs and listen to your inner self. Above all, enjoy your Tarot time.

DAY 1
Your Tarot pack

✛

Buying a Tarot pack

Many people use either the original Rider Waite or the almost identical but softer imagery of the Universal Waite Tarot pack. The Rider Waite pack is probably one of the most widely available packs and the names have been translated into several languages. But this book is not linked to any specific system and you can use any pack that corresponds to the order and symbolism of the core Tarot Major Arcana and suits. Some packs based on the Tarot may have a different number of cards and these can be confusing if you are new to the Tarot. You can, however, buy one of these for use as a tool for meditation.

Initially, you may find it easier to work with a pack with an illustrated Minor Arcana.

You will probably find that you are naturally attracted to a particular Tarot pack. When you look at the images, they seem instantly to make sense and not jar or seem artificial. To name a few, the Mythic Tarot uses Greek mythological figures, the Morgan Greer has brilliant colours and a fairy-tale quality, while the Aquarian Deck is another good beginner Tarot and is less ornate that the Rider Waite. But really it is a question of going to a New Age store or large bookshop and looking at the different packs and seeing which is right for you. Go to a store where you can handle the sample packs or at least see the full range of each set in a catalogue or book. You may be lucky enough to find a small, friendly New Age store that has a large range, where the people working in the shop actually love what they sell and will be happy to spend time with you, suggesting options. Though mail order does give a wide choice, where possible choose your pack personally. If you have been given as a present Tarot that you do not like or after a few weeks the pack you purchased feels wrong, explore alternatives, as it will become a special and essential tool in your spiritual work.

Make the day you choose your Tarot cards special and unhurried – no children, bored partners or boyfriends trying to rush you; this is not the time for a friend who has a shopping list as long as Oxford Street and a tight time schedule. Go alone or with someone you are comfortable with, for this is a day to dream and to be, not to do.

Making a special Tarot time and place

You can read Tarot cards almost anywhere, especially if you buy a scaled-down pack, for example the miniature Rider Waite. Over the past few years, I have given impromptu readings for strangers and new acquaintances on trains and ferries, at airports and office desks and in crowded TV and radio studios and cafés.

But when you work at home, it is good to create a special corner or room that is your Tarot place; it may be a garden chalet, a work room or a table in a screened or curtained-off corner of your bedroom. If you do read your Tarot in your work area, switch off your computer and any unnecessary electrical equipment and cover over reminders of unfinished tasks or unanswered correspondence. Try, if possible, to have a separate table for your Tarot work, your special place in which you can keep your favourite crystals, candles, oils and incenses. The new fibre optic lamps are particularly suitable as they cast a magical ever-changing glow. You should have flowers and cushions to sit on comfortably for meditation or contemplation, to make this a special place into which you can welcome those for whom you give readings.

Try and establish a special time too for your divination, so that at least three or four times a week you can set aside a segment of your life for your spiritual work, which need not necessarily centre around Tarot. This 'self' time is just as important as time you give to other people, for example ferrying a child to evening activities, doing aerobics or meeting the crowd in the wine bar. It is far more essential than household chores or giving time to people who make you feel bad about yourself. This is a date with your very best friend – yourself – and one you should try not to break unless absolutely necessary. If you do not want to do a reading, turn the cards over and let the stories fill your mind as you sit by candlelight. Alternatively, visualise yourself entering one of the cards and exploring it, going through doorways, listening to the characters. Even if you can only manage five or ten minutes at the end of the day, it is the quality of the spiritual experience that is crucial.

Keeping a Tarot diary

Each morning you should choose two Tarot cards from the full pack to act as your guide for the day. A Tarot journal is a good way to keep track of the patterns of the individual cards you select each morning and also to build up a database of Tarot wisdom. You may also wish to note significant readings for yourself and others. This can be especially helpful if a predicted outcome seems unlikely or you cannot immediately identify a person or situation represented by a specific card in a reading. Events tend to prove such readings true, but it is easy to forget details over time and these successes do build up the all-vital confidence in your own intuition, both within the divinatory context and your everyday world. But, most importantly, your journal can contain sections on each card and when a new meaning emerges in a reading or through scrying you can note it down.

In the same way as you work with basic spreads, you will discover ways of laying out the cards that seem to work better for you than those I suggest. Or you may read of a different spread or be shown one by a friend. Spreads (card layouts) are created by individuals and tend to pass into books and teaching materials if a number of people find the format helpful. But whatever experts tell you, there are no definitive spreads and the simple layout you devise may work better than traditional and very complicated spreads such as the Celtic Cross that has little connection with the Celts apart from its approximate shape.

A loose-leaf folder to which you can add blank pages makes a good diary for Tarot or, even better, a Filofax organiser with a diary date section for individual cards of the day and notes about readings, which can help in building up significant patterns. If the diary shows Moon phases, you may find these correlate with the nature of your readings; for example, on the day of the Full Moon they may be brimming with action. You can add blank pages for card meanings and layouts. There are some beautiful Filofaxes on the market with silver or fabric covers.

Empowerment and protection

Once you have chosen your Tarot pack, spend an evening exploring it. On this first evening, light frankincense or sandalwood oil or incense, to promote psychic awareness, and a silver candle, the colour of the Moon.

You may wish to consecrate your new pack to make the cards uniquely your own, to endow them with psychic protection and empower them with the ancient powers of Earth, Air, Fire and Water that I described in the introduction.

Some people identify the Protectors or Protectresses of the Four Elements as the devas, highly evolved nature spirits that rule over the mythical elemental creatures who were believed by alchemists to reside in each Element. These devas are in formal magic called the Guardians of the Four Watchtowers and are placed at each of the four main compass points in a magic circle. Others regard these guardians as angels, either specific archangels or elemental angelic forces working for the purpose of magic and divination. The form that seems most relevant to you is invariably the most potent. I have devoted space to these four powers, because they are entwined in the Tarot in the four suits, as Number and Court Cards, and also because Earth, Air, Fire and Water are integral to many of the symbols within the Major Powers. In all these settings, it can be helpful to envisage them as natural forces.

The Angel of the Earth

You will find him or her in a beautiful garden surrounded by butterflies and fragrant flowers. If you know such a place, go there when it is quiet and the sun is shining; if not, visualise the setting, perhaps focusing on a vase of flowers. Many of the Tarot cards are set in gardens or with backgrounds of fields or hills.

This angel is intensely practical and kind. You may see him or her in the intricate form of a cobweb sparkling with dew. This is the guardian of animals, children and old people, all who are vulnerable and who will bring out your gentle, nurturing side and foster your patience with those who may seem irritating or who are unduly critical, perhaps because of their own unhappiness.

This angel will stand in the north of the Circle of Power, offering protection, and will empower your Tarot card readings with gentle wisdom, compassion and above all an awareness of what is possible and realistic, beginning where you, the questioner, are right now.

The Angel of the Air

Where else would you see this angel but in the clouds? Walk on a hillside – even one in a town or city will do – and look up and you will find this angel, eager to impart knowledge and stirring you to blow away the cobwebs in your life. This is the angel of intellect to whom you can pose all those questions about the universe, who will, by gently probing questions, encourage you to answer them yourself. Though this angel will never judge or criticise, somehow you are made aware that you cannot give less than your best to life.

This guardian stands in the east of the Circle of Power, offering protection, empowering Tarot readings with truth without illusion or false mystique and the promise of new hope and regeneration, no matter how dark the present may seem. Above all, he or she endows a Tarot reader with the ability to make connections and identify the underlying patterns expressed in a reading.

The Angel of Fire

You will see this angel in a candle flame or perhaps the dawn sky, the noonday sun or a particularly vivid sunset. But you will have to be quick, for this is the angel of action and enthusiasm, who will inspire you to heights you never imagined. He or she sees obstacles as a challenge and, like the midday sun, reminds you to enjoy happiness now and above all to seize the moment. He or she will not promise tranquillity, but will help you to aspire to ever greater heights and expand your horizons.

This angelic guardian stands in the south of the Circle of Power and offers protection, endowing any Tarot reading with inspiration and clarity, so that the symbols on the cards form stepping-off points for both divinatory and personal psychic evolution, and the solutions and alternatives suggested offer new unconsidered options to seemingly insoluble problems or areas of stagnation.

The Angel of Water

Look into a lake or stream at sunrise and see his or her image dancing in the ripples. It is this angel who gave rise to the Easter legend that if you look into water at dawn on Easter morning, you see the angels dancing. But you can see him or her any day in the sunlight if you look hard enough.

You will see this angel also in a moonlit lake – mysterious, touching your inner depths and awakening a yearning for something more. Day or night, this is the angel of positive emotions and empathy, not sentimentality or possessiveness.

This Guardian Spirit stands in the west of the Circle of Power, offering protection and bringing intuitive insights to your Tarot work, so that the readings are healing experiences, suggesting solutions that reconcile and bring harmony to disparate aspects of life and disharmonious relationships.

An angelic/devic Tarot ritual

☉ Set out the cards of your entire Tarot pack clockwise in a circle, face uppermost, in order beginning with the Fool in the north of the circle (you can either find magnetic north or use an approximation for symbolic north) and ending to the immediate left of the Fool with the King of Swords standing sentinel over the circle.

☉ Sprinkle a few grains of salt into pure spring water and, with your power hand (the one you write with), beginning again in the north, create a circle of salt water just outside your ring of cards.

☉ Use incense to draw a circle of smoke just outside the salt-water ring. You have now created what is called in magic a triple circle of power and protection.

☉ Beyond the circle, so that wax will not drip on the cards, light a green or brown candle, the colour of the Earth, at the north compass point, to represent the Angel or Deva of the Earth or, if you prefer, another archetypal form of Earth power. Visualise the Guardian of the Earth emerging from the flame and standing sentinel.

☉ Light next a yellow candle, the colour of Air, at the eastern compass point and visualise the Guardian of the Air emerging from the flame and standing sentinel.

☉ In the south of the circle, light a red candle for the Guardian of the Fire and visualise him or her emerging from the flame to stand sentinel.

☉ Finally, in the west of the circle, light a blue candle for the Guardian of the Water and visualise him or her emerging from the light of the candle to stand sentinel.

☉ Sit quietly for a few minutes in the candlelight, letting the light of each power in turn, beginning in the north, extend its sphere and surround you with light and love. This light will strengthen your natural auric protection, the energy field surrounding us all, that manifests as colours, which can become weakened, especially if exposed to negativity.

❂ By creating a psychic short-cut to the Elemental Powers, you can invoke this power and protection at any time while you are carrying out Tarot divination or using your cards for spiritual development without repeating the ritual.

❂ Gaze once more at each of the Candle Guardians in turn, beginning this time in the west.

❂ As you do so, for each angel, touch the crown of your head with your receptive hand (the one you *don't* write with). This is the *chakra* (energy point) from which cosmic energy flows into the body. You may see this as a white ray, merging to violet.

❂ Now touch, again with your receptive hand, your 'Third Eye' or brow chakra, situated in the centre of your face just above your eyes. This is the psychic point at which the mind–spirit energies merge. You may see this as an indigo ray.

❂ Touch next the centre of your throat, seat of the throat chakra, with your receptive hand, seeing this energy as blue light, merging into turquoise from below.

❂ Now, cross your hands over your heart and feel the love and compassion seen as green light, drawing yellow power from below.

❂ Using your power hand, touch your navel, seat of the solar plexus chakra that absorbs positive energies from the external world and filters out negative ones. This you may see as yellow light.

❂ Next, touch your womb with your power hand, seeing the source of orange light rising from your sacral chakra, seat of desire.

❂ Finally, press your feet into the ground to maintain connection with the Earth, feeling brown/red colours rising to the base of your spine or root chakra before spiralling to join and empower the higher colours.

❂ Blow out the blue candle, then the red, yellow and green.

⊛ Continue in an anticlockwise circle, making your symbolic connections with your psychic energy centres and absorbing the light of each guardian as you extinguish each candle.

You can invoke your Elemental Guardians at any time by unobtrusively tracing the energy patterns (chakras) on the palm of your hand or with your fingers on a table, visualising the light enclosing you. If you are alone or with friends, you can touch the symbolic chakra points on your body.

Open the channel to your power and protection each time before you begin a reading and close your energies by visualising the protective light fading and reversing the order of the gestures.

Crystal protection

For alternative or extra protection whenever you give a reading, you can place crystals either in the corners of the room or at the four corners of the table on which you are working, to act as a psychic shield from any unintentional negativity. Protective crystals include: black agate, amethysts, bloodstones, carnelians, garnets, black and red jasper, lapis lazuli, tiger's eye, topaz and turquoise.

The Major Arcana 0–III

✛

Before you read the meanings of each of the 22 cards of the Major Arcana, even if you have used Tarot cards before, hold them one at a time and allow initial impressions to form in words or pictures. Certain cards may evoke a sense of joy, optimism or peace or even a sense of urgency. These feelings arise in the same way that you can look at a beautiful painting and understand its significance without ever studying an art history book: information helps you to appreciate the context and detail, but essentially the significance is personal, linking with the universal and personal mythological system we first consciously acquired as children, in fairy tales.

The Fool

The Fool is the first card in the 22 cards of the Major Arcana representing the essential self. The card may be numbered 0, 1 or even 22, depending on the pack, which is not strange if you regard the cards as a constantly evolving cycle of experience, giving many stages in a single lifetime (or, as reincarnationists say, over many lifetimes) in the evolution towards more perfect understanding.

The Fool is the most exciting, though potentially challenging, card in the pack, for when this card appears, especially when numbered zero, anything is possible, but to attain this new stage involves a step into the unknown. So it is that the Fool is usually depicted stepping or dancing off a cliff or rock, but not falling; and so it is depicting a deliberate decision, to go against conventional advice and even logic and follow intuition. This is not a leap into the dark, rather a leap into the light, whether that involves a minor but crucial change, or a major life review. This initial leap may be followed by dozens of smaller steps, sometimes backwards or sideways, that may involve an inner rather than external evolution.

In most packs the Fool is accompanied by a dog, a symbol of the instinctive awareness we all possess to guide us along our unique path. In myths, fairy stories and shamanic journeys, friendly animals represent primal intuitions. This power was demonstrated by Australian Aborigines who traditionally crossed their vast continent, guided not by maps but by Song Lines, the sacred grid of songs and legends associated with their special sites and natural landmarks. So too could indigenous sea-going peoples, living in the southernmost isles of Oceania, navigate oceans without the aid of a compass even on starless nights. Women are naturally in touch with these profound primal instincts. I have come across many cases of women who telephoned their mother or best friend at exactly the time when she was unhappy or in trouble but was telling no one of her distress. Mothers routinely wake in the night before an infant or sick child does and even when they are hundreds of miles away may know that a child is in danger.

However, it can be difficult to trust intuition in an age where logic and left-brained thinking is valued and a businesswoman is expected to be hard-headed and rational. Yet intuition, as symbolised in the Fool card, is every woman's friend and right now whatever your age or status, in work or personal life, the safe option is not the path to fulfilment or success on the stock market.

Tricia is in her sixties and married; she took her leap in the dark when she went on holiday to Egypt alone, to explore a past life connection she felt. For Kate, a single parent in her thirties, it meant taking out a second mortgage on her home and uprooting her family from London to a remote area of Cornwall to set up a holistic centre where women with young children would be welcomed.

The challenging aspect of the Fool is in the courage Tricia and Kate needed, the sort of courage you need if you are not unhappy in your present world, but have a yearning for something more, to make a change that those close to you cannot understand. Remember, they may resist the change simply because it will disrupt their own secure world.

The Magician

The Magician is the archetypal creator/trickster, known throughout history as the initiator of change and the spark that inspires action. But though he is the teacher of the Fool, akin to Merlin, wizard of Celtic legend, or Thoth, the ancient Egyptian god of wisdom and learning, the Magician teaches by posing challenges and directing the Fool towards necessary experiences.

In many Tarot packs, the Magician, who possesses strong animus (male) energies, has symbols of the four suits of the Minor Arcana on his table, representing the four elements from which the fifth, Ether (spirit), is created, bringing into actuality the new dreams and desires. So this is the card of creativity in any and every area of your life.

The Magician is a very powerful card for women, providing the impetus for innovation by sheer energy, enthusiasm and not a little magic. Associated with sexuality, this card indicates a woman who is in control of her own body, who may choose to have sex or be celibate in a relationship and does not need to use sexual manipulation to achieve her needs.

So it is a card that says you should use your own strengths to put your plans, great or small, into action in the immediate future, rather than seeking the help or approval of others; have confidence in your ability to live life on your own terms. Helena, who is in her late twenties, realised her Magician energies when she created a position for herself in management by combining a number of responsibilities she had taken over informally and drawing up a proposal for greater efficiency through her promotion. Alison, who is in her late forties, utilised her Magician when she stopped reading about astrology, a subject that had fascinated but intimidated her with its many facets. Instead, she began to cast horoscopes for friends and colleagues, having finally installed what had seemed an impossibly complex program on her computer, and modified it for her needs.

The only negative aspect of the Magician appears when the trickster element may tempt us to use manipulative means, such as pretending to be helpless, to achieve a goal, rather than relying on our own creative energies that may take longer.

The High Priestess

THE HIGH PRIESTESS

The High Priestess, the card of the separate self and of detachment, is the archetypal Divine Virgin, said in many cultures to be the weaver and the keeper of the sacred patterns that give form and order to the universe and to the lives of humankind.

She is associated with the maiden and the virgin goddesses such as Artemis, Greek goddess of the waxing moon, or Celtic Brigid in her maiden aspect, patroness of healers, poets and smiths. In some packs she is called Juno, wife of the supreme Roman god Jupiter, seen as the abstract, wise feminine principle of divinity rather than the sensual Mother Goddess.

Whether you live alone or are happily married or in a permanent relationship, she is the 'separate you', marking the divisions between you and other people, your loved ones, friends, colleagues. It is the card that does not fear but rejoices in our self-containment (a separateness which is inevitable from the time we leave our mother's womb). Her detachment is not indifference, but almost a Buddhist awareness that overdependence on power, success, the approval of others or material possessions will hold back our spiritual development

So you may need to explore what would fulfil *you* and make *you* rather than others happy; you need to develop your psychic and spiritual side and, no matter how busy and successful you are, make time for those quiet times when you connect with the natural, slower, cyclical female rhythms (more of this in the Moon card).

Meena encountered the High Priestess when she decided not to marry the wealthy successful man selected by her parents from her own traditional cultural background, but to support herself with an evening job and complete her studies. Sarah's High Priestess reminded her that the constant strict diet she followed to maintain her weight, in order to succeed as a dancer, may have helped her to fulfil an ambition that had been fuelled from childhood by teachers and relatives, but it also made her constantly feel an unattractive failure, because she was not a top-class dancer and was naturally well-rounded.

The only negative aspect of the High Priestess appears when detachment makes her indifferent to the needs of others and intolerant of their weaknesses.

The Empress

This is the card of the archetypal mother, the card of birth that, like the good fairy, offers the antidote to the Death card. This is the card of the ancient Egyptian god Isis with the infant Horus, the new Sun God. It represents Mother Mary with baby Jesus, Light of the World and all the Earth, and Mother Goddesses of different civilisations, bringing fertility, abundance and, at its most positive, the mutual interchange of unconditional love and giving.

In many Tarot packs, the Empress is pictured surrounded by corn, fruit and flowers, and may be seen in the full flow of pregnancy in

THE EMPRESS.

the aspect of the early mother statues. It is, therefore, a very welcome card, setting you (or whoever the questioner may be) at the hub of a network of relationships and creativity in tangible ways.

Of course, the relevance of the Empress is not restricted to mothers with a baby at each breast and an oven filled with Mom's home-baked apple pie, but also represents creative giving, caring and nurturing, whether of ideas, projects or people at home, work and in the wider world. It promises the fruition of projects, family joy, the consummation of love and a sense of being fulfilled through connection with others; it may be revealed in friendship or in a formal or informal caring role towards people, especially younger ones, or animals or the environment.

Kate's Empress was manifest when she edited and shaped a whole new range of books written by first-time authors, which succeeded largely through her own extensive input into the initial stages. Vicky, who found herself unexpectedly pregnant 20 years after the birth of her first child, decided to work from home as she felt she had missed out first time round on her baby's early development.

The negative side to the Empress only appears if love turns to martyrdom, or sours and becomes possessiveness. What starts out as giving out of pure love or friendship can end with exploitation or unhealthy dependency so that you lose sight of your own needs and identity (more of this in the Queen cards).

DAY 3
Beginning Tarot readings

✚

It is important to begin Tarot readings as soon as possible, so that you gain confidence in your abilities. The 'imaging' process you use in these early, purely intuitive Tarot readings is one of the most important keys to even advanced divination. In the introduction, I mentioned how you could use individual Tarot cards for scrying, the technique that is used when pictures that appear in tea leaves, in wax or ink on water link together. It is just as easy to read a whole spread by this means, letting the pictures form interconnected webs.

Reversed cards in readings, i.e. those dealt upside-down, are interpreted by some traditional clairvoyants as having a weakened or even reverse meaning from cards that are the right way up. However, while psychokinetic energies would seem to influence our choice when we select cards from a shuffled pack, in practice many cards are reversed as they are returned to a pack after a reading. From my own experience, each card has an innate positive and challenging aspect. It is usually clear, from the other cards that are drawn, when the challenging aspect becomes significant in specific readings, but even in this instance, it always offers an impetus to overcoming any such obstacles, not a warning of disaster.

Very often, in an unstructured layout of three or six cards, one card may appear particularly significant and the questioner will identify it as being of special importance. They will choose it first, quite instinctively, even when it was not the first card dealt. This card is known as the key card.

Some cards naturally contain more animus (male) energies, for example the Emperor and the Kings, and so are traditionally regarded as 'male' cards although these energies apply equally to women and may refer either to the need for assertiveness in a particular situation or to a man who is featuring significantly in a particular area or phase of life. However, some, for example the Fool, are either male or female and usually refer to the questioner.

Your first Tarot reading

Shuffle the first 22 cards, the Major Arcana, and set them out, face-down, in a circle.

- Allow a question to form or, if one does not come naturally, clear your mind and let the cards tell their own story.
- Turn over three cards from anywhere in the circle that feels right. Take your time and weave a myth around the images as though you were telling a story to a child. If this feels incomplete or you do not understand the significance, turn over more cards, up to nine in total.
- If the answer still is not clear, place the selected cards under your pillow, having looked at them for a final time just before sleep. The meaning will come in your dreams or early the next morning.

Selecting your card of the day

Each day, preferably in the morning, you should shuffle the whole pack, lay it out, face-down, and choose two cards.

The first card will highlight areas, opportunities or challenges that will emerge during the day. The second will suggest particular strengths, strategies or solutions. Although you have only learned four specific card meanings, you can use the images of unknown cards to trigger ideas and options.

You may find that these interpretations vary slightly even if the same card is picked on consecutive days, as the prevailing energies change.

The Major Arcana IV–VII

⊹

The Emperor

The Emperor is the card of earthly dominion, the ultimate animus or power card, the supreme authority figure before whom all bow; he is the All-father of many traditions, Zeus in classical mythology, Odin, the Wise One of the Norsemen, or Woden in the Anglo-Saxon tradition. He is frequently pictured enthroned in battle dress, for he is a courageous general as well as leader of his people.

THE EMPEROR.

The Emperor is an important if not naturally empathic card for women, representing assertiveness, ambition and the courage to stand against second-rate treatment of them, their loved ones or vulnerable colleagues or friends. Insecure men fear strong women, branding them unfeminine because they are prepared to work for what they want and not play helpless or flatter a guy's ego at work or in relationships. And so this card may appear when you need a surge of power or ambition, especially if you encounter the 'glass ceiling' in your career. Equality laws have righted some injustices, but have also driven many male chauvinists to adopt guerrilla tactics and close ranks in the workplace. But the Emperor has many positive roles, from complaining about shoddy service in stores or restaurants to taking on a paternalistic bureaucracy (more of this in the Justice card).

Francesca's Emperor appeared when she organised a successful legal protest against the building of a motorway access road that would have destroyed the habitat of rare local wildlife, although her future father-in-law stood to gain financially if the deal had gone through. Tess's Emperor was manifest when she told her manipulative adult son that she was no longer working overtime to maintain him and subsidise his perpetual student lifestyle and partying, at the cost of her own headaches and insomnia.

The Emperor is so positive that he is bound to have a strongly negative aspect. We all know – and may be intimidated by – someone who is impossible to please. The Emperor in this guise is not necessarily a man. It could be your mother, your mother-in-law, a tutor at college, your boss, even a friendly neighbour or your best friend who is digging under the foundations of your confidence. Learn to stop sacrificing at the Emperor's altar – you do not need the approval of this impossible taskmaster.

The Hierophant

THE HIEROPHANT

The Hierophant, another symbol of animus power, represents tradition of all kinds and accumulated spiritual wisdom. In the classics he is Saturn or the Saxons' Seater, the god of limitation and fate. In some packs he is called Jupiter, the Roman name for Zeus, the great god of the Greeks. His wisdom is that of conventional and learned insight, gained through application. He is the brake on pure inspiration, who demands you muster your facts and figures, so that you can make an informed choice.

The Hierophant can be quite a difficult concept for some women, myself especially, who usually rely very successfully on intuitive abilities and a personal direct, access to magic and spirituality, plus a measure of glossing over the harsher realities or omissions. But the wisdom of ages is not to be scorned, whether you are reading the background of any subject from reincarnation to the taxation system, filling in forms and emptying the in-tray, or seeking advice from those who are wise and not just self-important. I am writing this just days before my personal Hierophant, Hector the UK taxman, demands that I transform all my pieces of paper and crumpled receipts into a semblance of accounts and send him the large cheque that I was supposed to have saved in a separate account and not dipped into when the grocery money ran low.

Above all, you may need to listen to your Higher Self, the wisest guide of all, whose words may demand a high standard of conduct. For Jenny, her Hierophant led her to follow a course in reiki healing as she found it hard to direct or control her own natural healing abilities. For Linda, the Hierophant involved a realistic assessment of her use of her pack of credit cards that consumed a large proportion of her salary in repayments and left her constantly overdrawn and borrowing yet more to keep up with the spiralling interest.

Like the Emperor, the negative aspect of the Hierophant is quite fearsome. I call him or her the 'traffic warden in your head' who can pop up every time you contemplate parking on one of life's double yellow lines. All your hidden guilt feelings manifest themselves in headaches, high blood pressure and food binges, but you keep smiling because you must be a good mother, a good wife, a loving partner, a good friend, a competent member of the team even when deep down you know you can't.

When did the Hierophant first come into your life? Perhaps it all started with trying and failing to please the Emperor of your childhood. Remember how your brother got away with murder while you, as little sister, had to be quiet and tidy and always smiling? And who ended up seething inside and not blaming other people but accepting it as 'all my own fault'? So, over all those years since you started to believe all those messages about your own unworthiness, you've collected quite a snowball of guilt for the unhappiness or unresponsiveness of others. What keeps the Empress going in the service of others when she's really exhausted – carrying the guilt of all the people she's failed to make happy? No wonder she looks a bit manic in some packs.

Stop accepting the guilt loaded on you by others and listen to the positive voices of today (lots more of this in the Death and Judgement cards as this unnecessary sense of guilt and failure is for many women probably their greatest burden).

The Lovers

This is the card of duality, relationships, especially in love and matters of identity.

In any pack this card represents the issues of choice in relationships. These may involve a decision to become committed, marry or live together as long as love lasts, have a child or divert maternal instincts into equally fruitful fields; or to live alone, separate or divorce; or to remarry after divorce or bereavement, to create harmony with step-relatives and the families of ex-partners or stepchildren. Generally, the card charts the progress of specific relationships, especially in areas where there are questions of separate identity within the relationship.

It is hardly surprising that this card appears so frequently in women's divination, since women tend to be the glue in relationships, the one who keeps disparate people and their egos in what passes for togetherness. Left to their own devices, many guys would either tear one another limb from limb for possession of the dominant female's attention in the family cave or wander off to indulge in male bonding rituals such as drinking and watching football matches.

In some packs the Lovers card depicts the innocent Adam and Eve before the Fall, who did not need to hide their bodies, together with a third party, either Venus, goddess of love, or Cupid, or someone offering a choice, possibly between partners or perhaps between earthly and spiritual love. Originally the Tarot Lovers were a family group with a child between them.

So while this card may herald new love or a relationship that will deepen, it may equally indicate existing relationships at a time when they need attention or seem less than satisfactory, perhaps because of false expectations. For Hilary, who was divorced and in her late thirties, the Lovers appeared in her reading when she had to choose whether to give up her own successful career to follow her new serviceman partner who was being posted hundreds of miles away across the US or to pursue the relationship over a long distance. For Meg, who was single and in her mid-twenties, the Lovers revealed her decision to end an office affair with a colleague who had no intention of leaving his wife, a relationship that was causing tension in the workplace among the close-knit team in which they both worked.

The negative aspect of this card appears when there is a conflict of priorities, perhaps between a new partner and existing children, or between parents and a partner, or between two different friends who each resent the attention paid to the other, leaving you suffering the worst of both worlds (more of this in the Hermit and the Two cards).

The Chariot

The Chariot is the card of travel, change and ultimately triumph, of choosing the way and changing direction. So it is a potentially exciting card to appear in any spread, whether the questioner is a young woman who is leaving school or home for the first time or a much older woman who is perhaps for the first time determining her own destiny. For this is a card full of movement, both physical and emotional that may involve a change in lifestyle or perspective.

Mythology is full of heroes in golden chariots, such as Apollo, the Sun God, who daily rode across the sky. But we must not ignore their equally dazzling female counterparts, for example Sol (or Sunna) of the Norse tradition who rode her Sun chariot drawn by the horses Aarvak (the Early Waker) and Alavin (the Rapid-goer), with a golden shield to protect them from the heat of the sun, and the earthly Boadicea, or Boudicca as the Romans called her, queen of the Iceni at the time of the Roman invasion of Britain, who fought to the last for her people.

So this is a card of courage and of balancing different needs and demands creatively. In different packs, black and white horses, sphinxes or even cats pull the Chariot, as the rider strives to harness opposing powers and needs to maintain the impetus in order to succeed. For this is a card of questing, whether it is for a personal Holy Grail or to push further back the boundaries of possibility – and so it can seem a threatening card for those who would like us to remain predictable and static.

For Miranda, a widow, her Chariot card was manifest when at the age of 65 she shocked her children and grandchildren by refusing to organise the family Christmas as she had done for the previous 30 years, and went skiing alone. For Angela, the Chariot confirmed her decision to retrain as a counsellor after many years of running a business that was successful but no longer bringing her any satisfaction. She appointed a senior manager to take her place and enrolled on a two-year diploma course.

What is the negative aspect of the Chariot? It usually involves a tendency to keep changing the external circumstances when the problem is within, moving the old play to a new theatre with a different cast. This is especially the province of men who may change partners when the initial passion fades. But women too may find that love affairs, friendships and even jobs keep running into difficulties at the same point over the years (more of this in the Aces) and it may be that internal rather than external change is the key.

The Major Arcana VIII–XI

✛

Strength

Strength can be either card eight or 11, depending on how your pack is numbered. In this card, also sometimes called Force or Fortitude, a woman is shown closing or opening the mouth of a lion. She is Cyrene, a maiden of Artemis, goddess of the waxing moon, whom Apollo the Sun God saw fighting and winning a battle against a lion. As a reward he took her to the realm of the gods. Some packs show Heracles (or Hercules) wrestling with the lion.

STRENGTH.

The woman is sometimes also portrayed as the female Magician and so this is a card that goes far beyond issues of strength into female power. Strength is a card primarily associated with persistence, rather than aggression, and indicates that persuasion, compromise and just sticking out a situation or course of action can be more effective than dramatic actions or walking away from less-than-ideal circumstances.

Linked with this is the almost magical physical power of women, which is displayed when mothers lift cars off their children or save them from injury by almost superhuman strength. I have many attested cases of maternal strength in my own books, and in a real crisis women often display a degree of courage and altruism, especially for loved ones, that defies rational explanation.

In the everyday world, many women display a natural ability to persevere, whether with a difficult child, an insecure partner, an unwelcoming set of in-laws, a sarcastic colleague or an ungrateful elderly relative, recognising that unhappiness may lie at the root of unpleasant words or inconsiderate behaviour. So, too, will she struggle to honour work commitments, even though she may be nursing a broken heart or an illness that would have the average male executive seeking the bosom of a surrogate mother to feed him a boiled egg and 'soldiers' and warm his bed socks.

So Strength, perhaps the most reassuring if not exciting card, promises that by weathering a rocky patch in a relationship or an apparently unrecognised period of effort at work, you can win through. But this does not mean that you should give way to intimidation or emotional blackmail, whether it be from officialdom or an overgrown playground bully at work or at home.

Moira's Strength card emerged when she was struggling with a home degree course while bringing up two small children, having discovered she was pregnant for the third time and was due to have the baby a week after her finals. She looked at how far she had come and how she had achieved high marks even when she had been suffering from postnatal depression and she determined to continue.

Sophie's Strength was manifest when she was sent by the Royal Navy to serve on a ship where many of the older men were sexist and very resentful of having women on board. She conducted herself with quiet dignity, refused the advances of a senior officer who tried to seduce her and eventually gained promotion and a chance to help other women who were being similarly harassed.

So what is the negative side of Strength? It's the side of you that insists on being cheerleader almost permanently on show for an ungrateful world, and pouring love and effort into those who will never try to help themselves. Use your Strength to walk away.

The Hermit

This is another card to which some women, myself included, initially find it difficult to relate. The Hermit is the silent wanderer, standing apart from the world. Yet he is an integral part of us, our inner voice, that still, centre of calm within us all, which can be reached by temporarily moving away from the world and looking inwards to the world of dreams and visions.

In many packs, the Hermit appears in a monk's robes, carrying a lantern through the mist, sometimes on the mountain tops. The Hermit is identified as Hermes Trismegistus. He is the semi-mythological Egyptian sorcerer and magician who was said to hold within himself 'three parts of the wisdom of the whole world'. His magical secrets were hidden for many years and even when they later reached the West were kept shrouded in secret by the alchemists.

The Hermit is our Hidden Self, beginning in the personal, unconscious mind and penetrating deep into ancient, collective wisdom. These are the insights that come through being rather than doing, and in stillness rather than in action. In today's world, even young children are stimulated from the moment they can walk, with an incessant round of clubs and organised activities, and may not ever be given the time just to walk in the woods, play with sticks, stones and flowers and weave magical worlds in their imagination.

So if we can step back from the quarrels of others, in which we are acting as peacemaker, and from the conflicting advice and opinions all around, and listen to our own inner wisdom, then we will instinctively know the right words to say and the right course to follow. Access to the wisdom of the Hermit lies in walking in quiet, natural places and letting the waves and the trees in the wind speak to our inner self, so that we can regain connection with the primal voice that is wiser than any guru or volume of esoteric wisdom. The appearance of the card suggests a period of rest and quiet contemplation and letting-go of worries that seem to have no immediate solution, so that they can be refined and reformed – and hopefully resolved.

Tanya's Hermit emerged when, after a stressful period as a junior doctor in an accident and emergency department, she chose to spend her two weeks' leave alone at a spiritual centre, rather than going to an under-30s holiday complex in Greece with her friends. Though she knew she would enjoy the non-stop partying, she also knew it would leave her even less prepared for the weeks ahead on duty.

Suzy's Hermit appeared when, after 20 years, she stopped acting as peacemaker between her mother and her adult sister and refused to listen to each one's complaints about the other or carry barbed messages between them, a task which usually resulted in her bearing the mutual hostility. To Suzy's surprise, her long-standing problem with eczema cleared up in about a week.

The negative side of the Hermit lies in ignoring problems that do demand action and hoping that they will go away – this is very different from either creative or tactical withdrawal and usually results in even more stress when we do finally emerge from seclusion.

The Wheel of Fortune

The Wheel of Fortune varies in the different packs, the difference being in who is turning the Wheel. In some it is the blindfolded goddess Fortuna, suggesting that humankind is subject to the whims of Fate or that perhaps there is a higher law controlling our destiny that is hidden even from the deities. Others show the Egyptian jackal-headed god Anubis, conductor of dead souls, or the Egyptian god Amon, controller of destiny and life, who is linked with the Sun god. For the Wheel of Fortune is also the Wheel of the Sun and the endless cycle of the changing seasons and the constellations who give their names to the birth signs in astrology; so our Fate may be linked to the old saying that there is a season and a time for every purpose under heaven.

In Buddhist philosophy, the karmic wheel of birth, death and rebirth is turned by humankind's own actions in different incarnations. Therefore individuals can step out of destructive repetitive patterns by learning from mistakes and finding the still point that is both in and out of time, where our lives are not subject to the whims of Fate or driven by our needs and desires, but reach the point where we are truly in control of our destiny.

WHEEL of FORTUNE.

Modern women have far more choices than their grandmothers and great-grandmothers. However, even the best-organised life can be changed overnight by an unplanned pregnancy, a job offer that will require a major change in lifestyle, a person who meets your eyes across a crowded room and turns your ordered universe upside-down, a redundancy or unexpected promotion, an inflow of money or unforeseen expenses on car or home. It can feel as though the sudden turn of the Wheel has left you marooned on a rock or swimming for the shore through gigantic waves. You may not have the power entirely to choose your next step, but there is always some room for manoeuvre, even in the most seemingly inflexible situations and even the smallest positive reaction may be crucial to your future well-being. Mr Noah might have built the Ark, but you can be sure it was Mrs Noah who organised the animal fodder, shopped for provisions and asked the dove to bring back seasick pills and an extra packet of washing powder.

But the Wheel of Fortune card can also act as a psychic checklist, alerting you to expected and preventable hazards just over the horizon. For example, perhaps you have not been keeping your accounts up to date and the tax forms are gathering dust in a drawer as the penalties accumulate, or you are in the throes of a wonderful new passion and are not being as careful as usual with contraception, or you are flirting with someone even though you are still committed to another relationship. Sometimes we do subconsciously tip the Wheel by our own unwise actions and then blame nasty old Fate when events get tricky, ignoring our own collusion. In such cases, the answer is to acknowledge that you have been getting broody recently, or that a current relationship needs revitalising or consigning to the past. That way you take control for good or ill.

Kelly's Wheel of Fortune was manifest when she unexpectedly inherited her great aunt's small and dilapidated hotel in a remote but beautiful coastal area of New Zealand's South Island and decided to leave her well-paid but boring job in Auckland to open a small centre for watersports, her abiding passion. Ruth's Wheel of Fortune appeared during a period when she was consistently late for work and had been issued with several warnings. She acknowledged to herself that she hated working in a law firm that dealt mainly with wills and probate, with a group of chauvinistic males, and decided to go back to law school to improve her qualifications and get the job she really wanted, dealing with matters relating to children and families.

The negative side of the Wheel of Fortune comes when you allow another person, whether it is a fortune teller or an authority figure, to impose a fixed vision of the future on you so that you then unconsciously fulfil their prophecies.

Justice

This is a very powerful card, since it can act as an impetus for changing an unfair status quo and for establishing priorities and principles that define what really matters in your life – you as a person. Justice is invariably depicted as a woman, since many women naturally mediate and arbitrate in work and home situations. In many packs, Justice is pictured blindfolded, not because she is unseeing, as with Fortuna in the previous card, but so that she will not be swayed by external appearances.

Some packs show the traditional justice figure of Venus, goddess of love, holding the scales of Libra and the sword of Mars. Others show Ma'at, Egyptian goddess of truth and justice. In Egyptian tradition, after death a man's heart was weighed against the feather from the head of Ma'at. If the scales balanced, then the heart was free from sin and the deceased might pass to the after-life.

JUSTICE .

Traditionally the Justice card is associated with litigation and official matters and may appear in a reading when formal steps are being taken to resolve a matter. But in practice it usually refers to principles and ideals that are of importance or are being eroded at the time of the reading.

There may be an important principle for which you are fighting; perhaps it is to achieve real equality at work, rather than lip service to it; or to right an injustice, a bureaucratic blunder or an unfair slur on your name at work or socially. It is not a time to compromise, but to fight for what is important to you, however little support you may have, for you know you are right. Sometimes this can mean going through all the form-filling and seemingly endless stages of an official complaint or application – this is the frustrating aspect of this card – but in the end attention to detail, together with some of the persistence of the Strength card, with which it frequently appears, and a belief that the cause is ultimately worthwhile, will bring success.

Heather drew Justice when she was fighting for prompt, efficient and caring medical attention for her elderly father who had been waiting two years for a hip-replacement operation and was now confined to his home. Carole's Justice was manifest when she was falsely accused by an incompetent and jealous colleague of mislaying important documents. Carole went through all the old faxes, e-mails and office memos and was able to clear her name – a reminder that efficient record-keeping is an ongoing, if boring, part of the Justice concept.

The negative side of Justice is a tendency to repress your resentment about persistent but minor injustices, because you feel it would seem petty to complain. Try to identify areas where you are being unfairly treated and say, 'Well actually I do mind', or that wonderfully liberating word 'No', to the unreasonable demands of others, and claim your due credit. Otherwise the resentments may build up as an internal volcano until you suddenly react totally inappropriately to some innocent bystander, while the perpetrator of the injustice smiles sympathetically at your irrational outburst.

More Tarot readings

✛

Tarot readings do not have to be about dilemmas or even major decisions. Sometimes they are just a way of checking where you are on your life path and confirming you are still on track. In this way, Tarot cards are a tool for spiritual development as well as divination. But the majority of readings you do for friends and acquaintances will be triggered by the need to make a decision or a dilemma.

As with any other form of counselling, your function is to mirror the card meanings so that the person for whom you are reading draws the conclusions and makes the decisions. This is not as exciting as playing Wise Woman, and it is tempting, when someone is unhappy or worried, to promise better times or to advise him or her to give up what you can see is a destructive relationship. But whether you work professionally in the future as a Tarot reader or read only for friends, the hardest lesson, but the most necessary, is to learn to express your card interpretation and then to sit back and let the other person choose the path, even if to you their choice seems to herald disaster. The following reading is one I carried out several years ago; although Tracey used the full Major Arcana, she turned over only cards that you have met so far in this book.

Tracey's story

Tracey was in her early thirties and had at the time of the reading just left her husband, Ray. His overbearing ways and total irresponsibility with money had left Tracey bankrupt and lacking in confidence after the failure of their shop, which she had inherited from her father on his death five years earlier. Ray would never let Tracey handle the money side, though she has a good head for figures. He drank heavily with his friends every lunchtime and evening, and gambled regularly, spending any profits and leaving Tracey for hours on end to run the shop alone.

Tracey had, at the time of the reading, been offered a job managing a local shop and a flat was included with the job. Ray had asked her to let him move back in with her, promising things would be different. Tracey was reluctant to take her husband back, although Ray's family were pressurising her to give him another chance. She had no family of her own since her father died.

On the surface, Tracey's dilemma seemed clear-cut and for those who have never been in a destructive relationship, the only question must be why she stayed with Ray at all. But having myself been in a marriage where my husband so undermined my self-esteem that I truly felt I was the worthless, hysterical, incompetent woman he portrayed me as, I know that, especially with no family support, many competent and formerly feisty women take on all the guilt and blame for failure in relationships.

Tracey drew the Magician, the High Priestess and the Fool.

The Magician suggested that Tracey used her energies in her own service rather than that of others. She was feeling worn down by the pressures, but once she shed them, she could use the spark to rekindle her own life. Inside, she was still the powerful, creative person she had been before marrying Ray, but her energies had been diverted into Ray's demands and his manipulative ways, the negative side of the Magician.

The High Priestess reminded Tracey of her own inner strength and her separate self that could flourish, despite having become submerged in her marriage, making her see herself through Ray's eyes, as a nagging, incompetent shrew, instead of a woman under pressure not of her making. Her ability with figures and her organisational skills, which had kept her father's shop running for so long in spite of Ray's destructive attitude, would help her to succeed in her new job. For now, fulfilment seemed to lie through her own efforts and meeting her own needs and not in caring for others, least of all Ray.

The Fool implied that Tracey should trust her instinct on this occasion and not be swayed by the arguments of others, or emotional blackmail. Maybe she would need to make a step into the unknown; there could even be a third solution, which might involve moving right away once she had surfaced from all the problems that were engulfing her.

I met Tracey some years later, now running a successful chain of office equipment and computer retailers. After an initial period working in her new job and living alone in the flat above the store, she discovered that Ray had for some months been seeing an older woman. He had moved in with her, once it was clear Tracey would not consider a reconciliation. Though the divorce dragged on for years with Ray seeking to claim part of Tracey's salary, she finally became free and took a correspondence course in business and computer studies, eventually obtaining a good degree. She then applied for a bank loan to buy her first shop and since then business has continued to expand rapidly. Ray is now alone again.

Your own three-card reading

- ❂ Shuffle your cards from the Major Arcana, while thinking of a question or an area of concern and lay them out, face-down.

- ❂ Select three from anywhere in the pack and lay them, still face-down, in a horizontal row from left to right.

- ❂ Turn over all three cards and select one which seems to be the 'key' card and write down any images it suggests. The key card in a spread may not be the first one you dealt, but you will instinctively sense its importance. (See page 33.)

- ❂ Choose whichever seems to be the next most relevant card and continue the story of the first card.

- ❂ Now, examine the final card images and interpret the overall message of the three cards together.

If you are reading for someone else, hold and, if you wish, shuffle the pack yourself while talking to the questioner about any areas of concern or special interest in his or her life. Then allow the questioner to shuffle and lay out the cards, so that you both have your psychic imprints on the pack to create the right vibes for an interactive reading – the cards are acting as the medium for your joint psychic energies.

A Horseshoe Spread

You can use this spread with the Major Arcana, the Minor Arcana plus Court Cards or the whole pack.

This five-card layout assigns significance to the positions of the cards, in answering specific questions or issues. The spread varies according to different practitioners so if the assigned positions or the qualities they represent do not feel right, experiment until the format works for you. As with other readings, shuffle the pack while considering a question or area of concern and then deal five cards face-down in a horseshoe formation. Turn over all five cards.

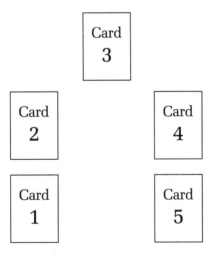

Read the cards in order, starting from the bottom left.

Unlike a three-card reading, the Horseshoe Spread does not have a key card (see page 33), but relies on the position meanings to build up the picture. However, card 1 may give a new perspective to the original question.

The significance of the cards

Card 1 The issue: This card indicates your present position and a choice, dilemma or predominant question about some aspect of your life.

Card 2 Present influences: These are all the people and circumstances that have contributed to your present position and that would be affected by any decision or change you make.

Card 3 Unexpected influences: These are partly the hidden factors that influence us, past successes, all the messages we carry from parents, lovers, etc. They also include those factors we can see just beyond the horizon that will come into play, according to whether we decide to change or preserve the status quo.

Card 4 Suggested action: This may indeed be action or possibly a conscious decision to wait. Either course will alter the path that we would have followed if we had let events or other people dictate the future.

Card 5 Possible outcome: This suggests the potential consequences of our intervention or decision.

As you have only learned some of the Major Arcana, use the intuitive method for cards you have not yet studied, allowing the images and associated ideas to guide you as to their meaning. The following reading drew cards you have already met from a full Major Arcana reading.

Chloe, an American in her mid-twenties, has been teaching media studies in England since leaving college and has recently been offered a job at a prestigious theatre school. She has become closely involved with Mel, an Australian who designed and built a lot of the stage sets, and Chloe's new job offered them the chance to travel round Europe together with the youth theatre company Chloe would be directing as part of her new post. However Mel, a committed Sai Baban, is anxious to use her carpentry skills to help rebuild homes for the refugees in Eastern Europe and she has already driven lorries on several aid convoys. She wants Chloe to go with her and help set up play schemes for the young children. Chloe is very happy in her world, but does not want to lose Mel.

Card 1 The issue: The Lovers

Hardly a surprising card, when for Chloe the choice seems to lie between love for Mel and her love of the theatre. If Mel will not compromise what she sees as her mission, Chloe must adapt to a life she regards as a waste of her own talents and one she would not fulfil well since she does not like children. This first card tends to state the problem as it is, which can make the choices seem stark, but allows a realistic solution to be found.

Card 2 Present influences: The Emperor

A card that Chloe identifies as Mel, for she says that Mel has always been very dogmatic about her charity work. I might have read this as being Chloe herself who wants to fulfil her ambitions, but that is why it is important in reading for others to encourage and abide by their interpretations, which are invariably right. This confirmed what Mel had stated the previous evening, that her own course was decided and that she could not compromise. Mel is convinced that her path is more worthwhile than Chloe's and that Chloe is selfish in not wanting to help the refugees. This is the core of the problem, for Chloe equally believes that the theatre fulfils an important function in bringing happiness and culture, especially to young people. Since her new post will be at a theatre school where there are excellent scholarships to help impoverished but talented students, Chloe feels that her work is important too.

Card 3 Unexpected influences: The High Priestess

Chloe had always, even as a child, wanted to work in the theatre and since coming to London had felt that she was able to express herself as an individual for the first time. Her own parents had devoted their lives to charity work; Chloe believed that this was at the expense of her brother and herself, and she had always been made to feel guilty for waiting to pursue 'frivolous activities' such as drama. Mel, albeit unknowingly, is pulling the same guilt strings and Chloe realises clearly for the first time that if she does give everything up to follow Mel, she would be betraying a vital part of herself.

Card 4 Suggested action: The Chariot

This indicates travel, but on Chloe's own terms. She is aware that if she follows Mel, she would not be fulfilling her own destiny but Mel's. So that would be a backward step, as it had taken years to get over her parents' disapproval of her lifestyle and priorities. But how could she maintain her relationship with Mel? Could the card be saying that absence might make the heart grow fonder or at least clarify their feelings? Perhaps Mel, too, needed to follow her own destiny.

Card 5 Possible outcome: The Hermit

Not a card suggesting immediate love, joy and happy ever after. Since Mel said that unless Chloe joined her, their relationship was finished, Chloe may well find herself alone. However, Mel may miss Chloe more than she realises now and on her home leaves they could perhaps re-establish another, different kind of relationship. The card does, however, promise that the solitary path will bring illumination and spiritual fulfilment for Chloe – we all have our unique path to what is of worth for us.

I met Chloe some months after this reading. She was very happy and her new job totally fulfilled her expectations – and more. Mel had gone off to Croatia, but had found her efforts to help rebuild the villages frustrated by bureaucracy. She was also very unhappy without Chloe. Mel made contact with Chloe on her return to England and they are slowly rekindling their relationship.

Tarot readings do not promise instant answers or happiness at the wave of a magical wand. Sometimes withdrawing from a no-win situation and waiting is the only way to allow time to bring about a natural resolution of a problem.

The Major Arcana XII–XV

⚜

The Hanged Man

The Hanged Man is in many ways the most profound card in the pack, linked with the voluntary sacrifice of the old King or Corn God, so that the new order can begin and fertility continue.

THE HANGED MAN.

Women are remarkably experienced in making sacrifices. In my research, I have come across many cases of women who gave their lives for their children, either in saving a child's life at the cost of terrible injury or death to themselves. There is also the less dramatic but no less noble sacrifice of women who give up their own happiness to care for a disabled child or a confused elderly parent or a terminally ill friend or relative.

The Norse god Odin is depicted in many packs; Odin hung on the World Tree for nine days to attain wisdom, until he finally saw the runes beneath him and, in reaching down for them, found he was free and reborn into enlightenment with no adverse effects apart from a stiff neck. So letting go is another way of thinking of the Hanged Man, whether it means letting go of redundant dreams, unrealistic expectations or avenues that are not fruitful.

This card usually appears when you have reached a crossroads and you have to decide whether to give up security, certainty or a destructive habit. Or perhaps you need to make an extra effort at work, or spiritually or in a relationship that offers no immediate gain. This is like the words from the Bible: 'As you sow, so shall you reap'. Three or six months down the road, perhaps even longer, you will realise that you made the right choice and will enjoy the benefits. However, now it may not be easy, whether you are supporting a troubled adolescent or depressed partner, studying after work, making time to understand the new technology – or even trying to cut down on fat and the sugars that you rely on for a quick energy boost.

Julia's Hanged Man was revealed when she left an extremely wealthy husband who treated her as a trophy on his arm, paid her an allowance like a child and expected her to be there morning and evening when he wanted clean clothes, a charming companion at business dinners or a sex kitten in his bed.

Paula's Hanged Man was manifest as a decision to work through her vacations from teaching, to help her partner start up his own business when his previous firm was forced to close during a recession after 30 years of trading.

What is the negative side of the Hanged Man? Perhaps you are sacrificing yourself for the wrong cause or becoming addicted to sacrifice, even for the best of motives – it's all too common. Danger comes when the giving goes on long after it is needed and the other person, too, gets locked into destructive dependency (hints here of the Empress, Strength and the Queens in their less positive aspects).

Death

Death is the card of natural change, that has somehow earned the most evil, yet undeserved, reputation. But believe me, **there is absolutely no way that turning over the Death card means that you or anyone close to you is going to die.**

Death is in fact an empowering card, a symbol of rebirth, beginnings after endings and renewal in more perfect, permanent form, in whatever aspect of life it touches. Death cards can be quite beautiful and spiritual, in some packs showing the mediaeval Grim Reaper, with his scythe, as a black skeleton or a knight in black armour with a skull revealed through the helmet.

In earlier times before organised health care dramatically reduced mortality rates in the westernised world, Death was a daily fact of life, as it still is in parts of the Third World, and so was not hidden away as a taboo. People would carry a *memento mori*, a talisman in the shape of a skull as a reminder to value every day and be aware that the spiritual nature of humankind is as important and more enduring than the physical form.

DEATH.

But the Tarot card talks of the hundreds of little deaths, the microcosmic transitions that we must undergo if we are to move forward, the 'death' of each stage in our life. So it is not predicting disaster, but rather indicating the need to close a particular door and move on to the next phase. This may be a mode of responding or a role that has become redundant and is blocking new growth. Of course, there will be regret, even at the most positive new beginning, for what is being left behind and for the choices that precluded other aspects of life or the personality, an ongoing theme in the Tarot.

Maggie, a single parent, met her Death card when her daughter started school and she realised that she needed to reassess her life, since she had put her career and adult relationships on hold while Emily was young. Joanne encountered her Death card when she was offered a scholarship at a French university, thousands of miles from home. She knew that she needed and wanted to accept, but regretted leaving her close-knit family and friends behind.

The negative aspect of Death shows itself when we do not accept the transition from one stage to another, as we gradually grow older. Even an 18-year-old has left behind her carefree childhood and there is nothing more tragic than an older women who strives to maintain her youth at any cost and does not value the deeper beauty that comes with wisdom and experience.

Temperance

TEMPERANCE.

On the surface, Temperance seems to be going against everything modern women have fought for, displaying patience and moderation more suited to a Victorian lady or at least Little Miss Perfect from your school who always handed in her homework early and remembered to label her games kit at the beginning of term.

But Temperance, in some packs in angelic form, in others depicted as Iris, goddess of the rainbow, speaks not of passivity, but of the harmony within you and the peace you bring to those with whom you live or work. As the messenger, she is the link between our mind–body and our Higher Self, between the conscious and unconscious worlds, the angelic being, the ideal self that lies within us all.

Temperance is actually a card of strength, not weakness, of accepting life as it is and people as they are. It means finding personal equilibrium, so that extreme joy and exhilaration are not followed by abject despair at the first obstacle or reversal. Some women are natural drama queens for whom life is an ongoing soap opera with constant relationship crises as each new best-ever friend or prospective partner turns out to have feet of clay.

This card talks of the need to avoid what may be extreme reactions in others. Sometimes you cannot be responsible for the happiness or success of others, nor in some instances can you change some people's unreasonable attitudes – you can only love yourself and create within you an oasis of calm and quiet joy that does not depend on the reactions of others. After all, Temperance, with her cousin the High Priestess and the Hermit, forms the trilogy of inner stillness. You should redress any imbalance or stress in one area of your life by making positive steps in another.

Concentrate on positive achievements and people who make you feel good. Value yourself even if someone else is undermining you.

Eleanor's Temperance card appeared when she finally accepted that the story of the prodigal son was for real. Having cancelled her own plans for skiing in Italy yet again at the request of her ever-complaining, but able-bodied, widowed mother, Eleanor found herself out in the cold after her sister Joyce jetted in from some exotic place for the weekend and assumed her place as the centre of their mother's universe. Eleanor rearranged her priorities so that she was no longer at the beck and call of her mother and moved home to be near the sea that she loved so much. Jenny's Temperance came when despite the long hours of unpaid overtime she had put in for months on the features desk of a national newspaper, the job she coveted was given to Andrea, a cousin of the editor's wife. Andrea spent her days in the office polishing her nails and quarrelling loudly on the phone with her latest boyfriend, but, instead of creating a scene, Jenny continued to work hard without complaint and finally secured a better post on a rival newspaper.

The negative side of Temperance is in getting out of touch with the real situation and so allowing bad decisions to pass without comment. Occasionally everyone needs to make a stand, even at the risk of temporary disharmony.

The Devil

The Devil, like the Death card, is sometimes feared in Tarot readings and seen as a premonition of evil or danger. Yet, like Death, it contains great potential for the release of positive energies if negativity can be acknowledged and used as the impetus for change and to overcome injustice or inertia. The Devil as a power to be eradicated is a Judeo–Christian concept. In contrast, in Oriental and some other Western philosophies, evil is the other polarity of good, and the gods of evil, such as Loki in the Norse tradition, were necessary for transformation.

Many of the Tarot Devil cards are based on the goat-footed pagan Pan, the horned god of nature. Mother Nature can be both creative and destructive and if there were no impetus for change, caused by dissatisfaction, we would all still be in our cribs 40 years on.

THE DEVIL .

Some women still fear anger in themselves and try to emulate Mother Teresa even when they feel like Kali on a bad hair day, pushing deep inside themselves any pent-up fury or resentment bubbling beneath the surface. Of course, it simply reappears hours or days later as a migraine or insomnia, or an irresistible urge to devour every a calorie-laden cream bun from the tea trolley.

Let your family, friends, lover or children know if you are feeling premenstrual, depressed or resentful rather than expecting them to second-guess from your sighs of muffled martyrdom; demand from others the consideration you give to them when they need nurturing. Big girls should cry and nice girls should yell now and again when people impose upon their good nature too frequently or assume that toddler tantrums can win arguments in the board room or on the shop floor as well as the nursery.

Annie's Devil manifested itself when her teenage son arrived home from university with a sheaf of unpaid final demands and a sack of dirty washing and helped himself to the contents of the fridge, before telephoning all his local friends to arrange his welcome home party in the local pub. Judy's Devil appeared when for the fifth year running her personal assistant telephoned work on the first day of the January sales saying she was in bed with a migraine. Next morning, as on previous occasions, she arrived in a trendy designer outfit, regaling everyone in megaphonic tones with tales of the great and glorious with whom she had shared pâté sandwiches in the overnight queue outside Harrods.

The negative aspect lies only in accepting less than considerate treatment from other people, because deep down we feel we merit nothing better. We may ensnare ourselves by our low expectations and so project our self-hatred on to self-created demons, giving others the power to put us down.

The Major Arcana XVI–XVII

✛

The Tower

The Tower of Destruction, the card of liberation from restriction, is another card that conventionally, but unjustifiably, has negative connotations. In most packs, it certainly is fairly dramatic, split open by fire and tempest. Sometimes it is called *La Maison de Dieu* which is not, as one might expect, 'the house of God' but a corruption of *Diefel*, the biblical Tower of Babel.

The Tower of Babel was built by the descendants of Noah in an attempt to scale the heavens to avenge themselves on God for sending the Flood. As a punishment, God sent down a confusion of tongues and henceforward it was said that different languages and misunderstanding caused discord among humankind. In fact, this was in itself a liberation so that diversity, not only of expression, but ideas, could germinate to prevent stagnation.

Even so, the Tower card does not augure future disaster, but reflects an inner awareness that, in some area of your life, restrictions or feelings of being stifled are clearing and suddenly there are new options or perspectives. Perhaps something that you might have initially regarded as a setback has given you an opportunity to rebuild an area of your life in a positive, more fruitful way, using your experience and wisdom to arrange the pieces, perhaps for the first time, in the way you want. The card can also indicate that you would like to split open a particular 'tower' yourself, one that offers security but holds you back from personal or spiritual growth.

Women are not usually ones to walk away from a reversal, whether of their own or other people's making. They try to see what can be salvaged. But sometimes it is important to use the Tower as a time for reassessment to decide what is of worth and what should be consigned to the past.

Jane experienced her Tower at the age of 20, when, after going out with the same guy since the second year of secondary school, just as her mother and future mother-in-law were buying their hats and arguing over the wedding guest list, she suddenly realised that she and David were just a habit. Jane was not ready to settle down to what had become premature middle age. Dave was hurt, and the families bewildered, when she decided that she needed time to grow up and find her own separate identity. She and Dave got over the initial bitterness and are now still friends and he too is considering a new career and moving out of his all-too-comfortable home.

Annette's Tower came after she had been made redundant at the age of 55 from the bank in which she had worked since leaving school. Rather than taking early retirement, she used her redundancy money to set up a herb farm and to finance a course in traditional Chinese medicine that had interested her since a holiday in Hong Kong.

The negative aspect of the Tower comes when the new beginning is built on the same shaky foundations that caused the original edifice to collapse – it is important to analyse the underlying causes, not least the frustrations that were experienced by the original Tower.

The Star

The Star is an image that is of importance both as the inner star of illumination and the guiding star towards fulfilment of tangible dreams. It appears in the same role as Tir, the Pole Star (see my book *Runes Talk to the Woman Within*).

Through our spiritual connection with the stars, we can experience what the Greek mathematician Pythagoras called the 'harmony of the spheres' or 'the music of the universe'. Astrology links each of us to a particular constellation. So the appearance of the Star in a reading is a way of saying that this is an issue close to your core self and that the blend of planets, linked with the constellations, reflects what you could become – and so right now your personal and cosmic energies are giving you extra power to take a step on that road.

The Star Maiden who appears in many packs does not even have clothes or material trappings or burdens to separate her from her connection with the natural world, and in some cards she gazes deep into a pool. 'As above, so below', runs the ancient maxim, and so your dreams and plans for the future are rooted in your own psyche, the inner world of your dreams and most importantly in the earthly or practical sphere, so have firm foundations.

This is the 'good fairy' card that says you can make your dreams come true, whether you are 18 or 85, by taking the first steps, however small, now guided by inner faith and drawing on the power of the natural world all around you to give you the impetus. This dream may involve developing your psychic or healing abilities, making a dazzling career leap, finally joining a drama group, writing your first short story or article, or living, either alone or with a partner, in a way that makes you feel complete. There are many stars in the sky and it is so easy to lose sight of our own special star, and end up following one that is right for others and brings happiness of a kind, but not the sudden burning glow that calls you to fulfil what is your private dream.

Gemma's Star involved getting a major part in a play with a repertory company, though she was severely dyslexic and had to learn her role from tapes. Alison's Star was manifest when on her seventieth birthday she shocked her family by moving to Italy to set up home with an Italian widower she had met several times on earlier holidays.

The negative aspect of the Star resides in refusing to settle for less than perfection and wishing your life away or living it through the achievements of others.

A reading with six cards

Reading with six cards is no different from a three-card reading, except in the additional scope it offers to explore an issue in greater depth. These unstructured readings are sometimes also called Gestalt Spreads, after the school of psychology that discovered that the whole is different from and greater than the sum of its parts. They build up a picture from the individual cards, so they are more flexible than a spread with set meanings, at time when an issue is not clear-cut and there may be several related areas that affect the answer to the original question.

Now that you have learned 16 cards, you will recognise many of the meanings if you use only the Major Arcana, though intuitive reading is still an important part of the process. The nine-card gestalt reading that you will use later in the book offers an even more detailed overview.

As before, you shuffle the pack and deal six cards, in the order shown overleaf, face-down. Turn all the cards over and identify which seems to be the key card (see page 33) and then allow your intuition to reveal the correct card order. Alternatively, you can read them in the order they were set out.

If you are reading for someone else, shuffle the cards first and then hand them to the questioner who can shuffle the deck while concentrating on a question and then deal them face-down. As with a three-card reading, the questioner will be able to identify the key card and the subsequent order of reading.

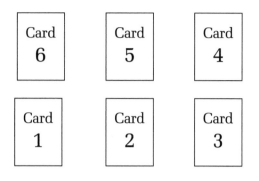

Linda, who is in her early sixties, has worked as a healer and clairvoyant for more than 30 years, writing several books and giving demonstrations all over the world. Her only daughter, Janine, married six years ago and lives nearby. However, Tony, her son-in-law, regards the psychic world as at best the province of cranks. Linda's granddaughter, Sarah-Jane, who is five, has started to talk about the people she sees standing round her bed, including Linda's late husband who died just after Janine was born, and this is making Tony increasingly hostile. Sarah-Jane is not at all afraid, but her father blames Linda for filling his daughter's head with nonsense. In fact, Linda does not talk about her work to the little girl. However, Sarah-Jane has asked several times about the light around her grandmother's head and the angel who stands behind her and Linda has explained about auras and angelic guides and how children are able to see them.

Linda has been told that she is no longer allowed to have her granddaughter staying at her home and Tony says that unless Sarah-Jane stops her talk of ghosts he will no longer allow Linda even to visit her grandchild. Janine is torn between her mother to whom she is devoted and her husband. Linda used the full Major Arcana and selected cards that have been met in the preceding chapters. She felt that the order in which the cards had been dealt was the order in which she wanted to interpret them.

Card 1 Justice
Linda naturally feels that she is being unfairly treated and that if necessary she would go to court to gain access to Sarah-Jane. She

is also angry that Sarah-Jane's natural psychic abilities are being treated so insensitively. The thing she finds most unfair is that Janine is not supporting Sarah-Jane, although Janine had similar experiences as a child and adolescent. So far Linda has not protested, but acknowledges in this card that the matter has shaken her to the core.

Card 2 Strength
This card counsels patience but persistence and suggests that Linda should quietly but firmly explain to her daughter the unfairness of the present situation and her concerns for Sarah-Jane who cannot understand why she can no longer stay with her grandmother. If this does not work, she may need to tackle the lion – Tony – and calmly state that while she respects Tony's right to determine how his daughter is brought up, he must equally respect that there are viewpoints different from his own. He should be sufficiently open-minded to allow Sarah-Jane to experience an alternative lifestyle where the emphasis is on spirituality rather than logic, both of which have validity.

Card 3 The Hanged Man
Because Tony is so fixed in his views and Janine will not stand against him, Linda may have to give up her natural desire to have her granddaughter to stay for a while, without expressing her justifiable indignation. Linda must make the most of the times she and the little girl do meet, in order to maintain what will be later a crucial relationship for Sarah-Jane if her parents cannot come to terms with her spirituality.

Card 4 Temperance
Another card that advocates patience and forbearance, Temperance advises a moderate approach so that Sarah-Jane will not feel a conflict of loyalties between her parents and her grandmother. Linda must continue, when asked by the child, to acknowledge her granddaughter's experiences as valid, for to do otherwise would be hurtful and would isolate Sarah-Jane and perhaps make her afraid of what other adults were denying. But

issuing an ultimatum, however much right is on Linda's side, would escalate an already difficult situation and so perhaps precipitate a permanent rift.

Card 5 The Devil

What negativity is being repressed or denied? Linda's own feelings are quite clear, so this obviously refers to underlying bitterness and tension beyond the explicit conflict. Linda explained that Tony had as a child lived with his aunt as his parents were divorced and from the early days of the relationship he resented Janine's close relationship with her mother. Although Linda tried to make him welcome, he has made it clear many times that he would prefer it if Linda, like his own family, confined contact to Christmas and birthdays. Since Sarah-Jane's birth, Janine has given up work and depends financially on Tony. Linda has watched with dismay as gradually Janine's confidence has been eroded as Tony criticised her mothering skills and insisted that Sarah-Jane made no mess when he was at home at weekends and was in bed when he came home in the evening. Janine is clearly depressed and Linda knows that Tony has hit Janine more than once, but Janine refuses to talk to her mother about the situation, or to seek the help her mother has suggested to deal with her depression and Tony's violence.

Card 6 The Empress

This clearly refers to Linda herself as a mother and grandmother and says that her love and wisdom are vital to Janine as well as to Sarah-Jane. All she can do is to see Janine and Sarah-Jane as much as possible when Tony is not around and to make it clear tactfully to Janine that she is there to help practically as well as emotionally and that she will offer a refuge if the violence continues. Like many readings, this one does not offer an instant solution, but promises that if Linda can wait and not compromise her own beliefs, while avoiding open conflict with Tony, then one day Janine may feel able to tackle and seek outside help for the real problems in the marriage that extend far beyond the issue of Sarah-Jane's magical experiences.

The Major Arcana XVIII–XIX

✥

The next two cards are of special significance since they are next to our Ascendant sign, the two major planetary influences both on a natal chart and by their movements on our lives. Women are more receptive to cosmic trends, though more men are beginning to open themselves to these influences. So the appearance of the Moon and Sun cards highlight, in the first case, the importance of your emotions and unconscious wisdom especially on inner matters and, in the second case, your current progress in the external world. Should the Sun and Moon both be drawn in a reading, you can call on both aspects of your wisdom and this augurs well for any matter. The Star, the Moon and the Sun in a reading is the most fortunate combination of all.

The Moon

The Moon is the quintessential woman's Tarot card and reflects the importance of dreams and of lunar intuitive insights and emotions even in today's factually orientated world. She appears in everyone's birth sign for about two days and so her influence will heighten your intuitive faculties on those days.

THE MOON.

What is more, living the Moon way is the route not only to the older, slower time that recognises the natural ebbs and flows of the female energy cycle, whether she is still physically fertile or not, but also to the world of spiritual and psychic awareness that is as important to stressed-out female executives as to the priestesses in the ancient Moon temples.

The Moon Goddess was worshipped from early times in her three aspects that reflected the life cycle of maiden, mother and Wise Woman: birth, fruition, death and then rebirth again, a cycle that is mirrored in the passing seasons. Artemis, or Venus, is the virgin goddess of the waxing moon, associated especially with Taurus; Selene, the mother, or goddess, of the full moon is linked with Cancer whom she rules; and the Wise Woman, the waning phase, belongs to the goddess of the harvest, Demeter, whose daughter Persephone was taken from her into the underworld and resides there for six months of the year, thus bringing winter. Demeter is linked with Virgo in her harvest aspect. Finally, Hecate is the Crone, hag of the night, embodying the wisdom of experience and an awareness of endings. She stands for the dark of the moon, associated with the period of Scorpio, when we cannot see the moon in the sky and must trust it has been reborn.

The Tarot cards reflect the cycles of the moon and the primeval untamed call of nature within us, that can make even the most sensible female kick off her shoes and run barefoot across the park and hug trees on the first day of spring or dance in puddles and laugh aloud with the sheer joy of seeing the sun rise over the sea on the first day of a holiday.

For now the inner world, the imagination and the instinctive inner voice are the best guides to action. If you listen to your heart and follow it, answers will come. If they are not clear, gaze at cloud formations, the dying embers of a barbecue or sunlight on water and let the images speak to you. Allow yourself to daydream, explore your psychic abilities. We are more than just creatures of the everyday world, and so if you let your inner world guide you for a while then you will, after a time, approach life with a new understanding and serenity.

Stephanie's Moon appeared at a time when she had been offered promotion that would involve her travelling abroad for part of the year. It would, however, mean leaving her daughter who was only 15. Although Claire could stay with her grandparents, as

Stephanie was a single parent and Claire's father was not on the scene, Stephanie felt instinctively that Claire needed her support and guidance as she was having a difficult time at school with bullies.

Veronica's Moon was manifest when she joined a healing circle and was having difficulties, not with understanding the theory, but with getting in touch with her innate healing abilities that she had used many times successfully with friends and relations. Veronica realised that that she was trying to rationalise healing and emulate the techniques of the more experienced healers, rather than allowing her natural energies to flow.

The Moon can only have negative connotations if it takes over and, as with the Star, you find yourself equating magic with immediate delivery of a gift-wrapped handsome prince with no dysfunctional relatives or alimony payments, who will whisk you away to a fairy-tale castle in the clouds.

The Sun

The Sun is the symbol of conscious power, clarity and drive, and with this card anything is possible.

THE SUN .

Though it is usually associated with animus power and the great solar deities, some cultures do have Sun Goddesses, who can outflank the guys. For example, among the Inuits, the Sun is pictured as a beautiful girl who carries her torch through the sky. The Sun and Moon are sister and brother Seqinek and Aningan or Akycha and Igaluk. Their path around the heavens is seen as a perpetual race in which the Moon, at first close to his sister the Sun, loses ground until she finally overtakes him at the end of his cycle, which explains why the Moon can be seen during the day.

In Lapland, the Sun Goddess, Baiwe, is also mother of the animals and at the beginning of February, when the sun returns, the women bake a special cake in her honour and hang it on the tent doors to ensure the favour of the goddess in the coming hunting season.

So this is the card of returning light, that at any time of the year represents pure energy, optimism, joy and success in the world's terms. It speaks of developing your potential, all the untapped or undeveloped talents and unique gifts you have, which promise that at any age you can still fulfil many of those dreams seen in the Star card.

The Sun is always a card full of golden light and brilliant colour, whether there is a new opportunity on the horizon or a resurgence of energy. For every one of you in whatever circumstances, the Sun card tells you to believe in yourself and love yourself; then whether your ambition is to grow beautiful flowers or to be president of the biggest bank in the world, you can and will succeed if you try hard enough.

Ingrid picked the Sun card when she decided to set up her own painting and decorating business from home, specialising in low-budget, personalised schemes that would create harmonious settings in community buildings as well as private homes, based on her knowledge of colour therapy.

Grace's Sun card manifested itself when, in the year before she was due to retire as head of a college art department, she had a chance to fulfil a life-long ambition to go Arizona and live with the Navajo people, studying their designs, in return for helping to set up a formal art education programme. She took early retirement and a reduced pension because she feared the moment might never come again.

Just as excessive exposure to the sun can be physically harmful, so it is important not to ignore entirely the consequences of concentrating single-mindedly on success – or confuse fulfilment with attainment.

A reading over nine days

Now that you have learned 20 cards, you will find that your daily readings are starting to form a coherent pattern. If certain cards appear, especially in the key card you select each day, it may suggest that certain areas of your life are of special importance. Repetition in the second card selected each day says that particular strengths or modes of action will be of help to you during this period. You may find that a particular card changes positions, thereby saying that it is an issue that contains an inbuilt resolution. Although the cards of the day are generally selected from the whole pack, some people divide the pack and use the Major Arcana to give the first card and the Minor Arcana plus the Court Cards for the second.

However, Elinor used only her Major Arcana cards for both of her daily choices, which some people prefer, and so attained a nine-day pattern that was made up of the first 20 cards that you have learned.

Elinor is in her late thirties and has had fertility problems. She needs to decide whether to continue with painful and frustrating treatment that has reduced sex to preordained encounters ruled by her ovulation chart. Peter, her partner, is 15 years older and already has a son by his first marriage. Peter admits that fatherhood first time round was a non-event as he was working away for most of his son's childhood.

Elinor is a veterinary surgeon and has been offered a chance to buy into the practice, which would involve taking out a heavy loan that would make it difficult for her to give up full-time work in the immediate future. She and Peter are arguing constantly about the rounds of tests and enforced love-making and he has been spending more and more time working late and coming home after she is asleep. Her nine day cards are:

Day 1 The Lovers and the Wheel of Fortune

Day 2 The Empress and the Sun

Day 3 The Devil and the Hermit

Day 1

The Lovers proved a significant card for Elinor as she was worried that her relationship had become focused around the fertility issue to the exclusion of everything else, and she was aware that for Peter another child was not a priority. The Wheel of Fortune emphasised for Elinor the fact that she was trying to tip the balance in favour of fertility that was eluding her naturally and suggested that perhaps if she could not allow events to take their course, she should at least draw back on what had become an obsession, albeit an understandable one.

Day 2

The Empress would seem to refer to her desire to be a mother, but Elinor said that she also derived a great deal of joy from working with animals and had immersed herself in her career during the last difficult months. The Sun augurs success if she put all her effort into achieving her heart's desire – but is this having a baby, becoming a partner in the surgery or both? The first day's cards had suggested she should allow nature to take its course, but I thought we should wait to see what the other cards revealed.

Day 3

The Devil does frequently refer to inner angst, rather than an obvious cause of negativity. So what negativity is lurking beneath the surface? Elinor said that she felt very bitter that Peter had a son with his first wife with whom now he has an excellent relationship and she feels illogically threatened because she has not experienced motherhood with Peter, though Peter left his wife for her. The Hermit suggests that Elinor needs to take time to examine her fears about her relationship with Peter and to assess whether these would be allayed by having a baby.

Day 4
The Chariot tends to refer to a personal change, so perhaps Elinor needs to decide on the direction of her life and turn her energies to the partnership, thus taking the spotlight off the baby issue that is causing so much tension between herself and Peter. The Lovers emphasises the need to work on her relationship with Peter to rekindle the pleasures they shared in the early years, so that whether or not they have a baby, they will have firm foundations for a continuing relationship. This is the second appearance of the Lovers within a short period and in the second position suggests that the solution lies within the relationship itself.

Day 5
The Sun and the Emperor are both power cards, auguring happiness and success for Elinor. This is the second appearance of the Sun card, again with a change in position – it was previously with the Empress. This is significant and says that it is Elinor's animus ambitious aspect that comes to the fore. This is not to preclude the baby, merely to change the emphasis. Elinor commented that Peter found it hard to accept her own vulnerability. He had complained many times that his first wife was boring and had been obsessed with their son and family life, so it is a reminder that it is as a powerful professional woman that Peter values her. This, however, may not be the role she still wants to maintain.

Day 6
When the Magician appears, something unexpected or exciting is afoot. To my surprise Elinor identified this immediately and for the first time became really animated. As well as the partnership, which did not excite her though it was a logical step, Elinor said she had been offered a chance to work on a local project for wildlife conservation, as the local wetlands were being reclaimed

from private ownership by a national charity. Her practice had offered her six months' sabbatical to set up the new scheme and monitor the migrating birds. It was something she wanted to do, but had not gone ahead as she thought that she might become pregnant and so the work, which involved overnight camps in the wild, would be too tiring. The High Priestess suggests that it is important for Elinor to re-establish her identity and confidence, which had become eroded by what she regarded as her failure to become a mother.

Day 7

Temperance says that personal harmony is important for Elinor as anxiety is counterproductive both to her chances of conception and to a positive relationship with Peter. The Star is a reminder of all the dreams Elinor had before she met Peter and before she wanted a child; these dreams are still part of her and can still be fulfilled. Elinor mentioned her love of wildlife photography and how she had always longed to publish a book of photographs. This was still possible, especially if she took part in the wildlife project. Motherhood was a goal for her but not her only one and the urge to have a baby can be so strong in some women that it may temporarily overshadow other equally vital aspects of their personality.

Day 8

The Lovers appeared for the third time, confirming that the relationship with Peter was the central issue – what each of them really wanted from the relationship – and that needed a great deal of discussion and perhaps a new direction. This was suggested by the Fool as a course of action. Elinor said that Peter also had wanted a change of lifestyle, to take redundancy from the large insurance brokers he worked for, which he felt was impersonal and did not really care about its customers, and to work as a freelance financial adviser from home. This was obviously risky and had been pushed into the background over the past few months. But it was still very important to Peter and so to the relationship.

Day 9

Elinor had chosen the Hanged Man: but what was the sacrifice? Elinor said she had been wondering whether to give fertility treatment a break for six months, as her consultant had suggested as she was becoming very stressed and her body exhausted from the drugs. What would be the result? Yet another Sun appears, promising ultimate happiness if she did make a short-term sacrifice.

Elinor continued to get similar cards over the following month and made the decision to leave fertility treatment for the immediate future and let nature take its course. She took up the wildlife contract and Peter went freelance. Their relationship regained its spontaneity and though Elinor was still anxious about the baby, she stopped feeling second-best to Peter's ex-wife. At the end of the six months, Elinor found that, against the odds, she was pregnant and Peter, to his surprise, was delighted. I met Elinor about a year later – she and Peter were sharing the child-care, something he had never done in his first marriage, and she had a permanent part-time position with the conservancy. Few Tarot readings have such storybook endings, but they can sometimes identify key issues and suggest solutions that can put a matter into perspective and draw together seemingly unrelated strands to allow a positive resolution.

The Major Arcana XX–XXI

✛

Judgement

Judgement is the card of reconciliation and spiritual renewal, though the symbolism in different packs may emphasise the aspect of the Last Judgement, the Day of Reckoning that permeates many mythologies and faiths in the West. However, St Michael, Archangel of Light, depicted on many Judgement cards, is in fact the Angel of Salvation, blowing his golden trumpet to restore life, in a more perfect and permanent form.

JUDGEMENT.

So Judgement is a card of resolution, drawing together disparate pieces. It speaks of unity with self and acceptance of the world as it is. The ancient Bone Goddess who predates formal mythologies took apart the shaman or deity and reassembled the bones in a perfected form, endowed with spiritual power and the ability to transcend time and space. Though these transformations took the goddess three days, for many women reconstruction of their lives after a major crisis or reassessment at a natural change point may take months or even years and can involve many blind alleys before being manifest as the integration of the World card.

The Judgement card is in a sense the time capsule into which we must step, leaving behind emotional baggage, regrets and attachments to the past that are no longer needed and fears for the future that may never materialise. If we can trust our own judgement, guided by the inner voice of the Hermit, and remain true to ourselves, as encapsulated as the High Priestess, then we can be truly free.

Judgement acknowledges that injustices from the past cannot be righted and that all we can do is to let them go. Most of us have at some time made truly monumental miscalculations that cause us to hide under the blankets even 20 years later when we recall every unwise word and hasty action. Compared with the average female, the elephant is absent-minded. Some relationships can be mended and some situations retrieved, but what cannot is best consigned to life's dustbin. What is even more important is that you trust your own judgement and play by your own rules, not those set by other people who may have their own game plan and agenda.

Louise's Judgement card appeared when she finally let go of her regrets that she did not take the opportunity to travel from Australia to London as part of a jazz band that later enjoyed moderate fame and fortune. Instead, she went to music college and is now a successful teacher. However, she has decided to rekindle her love of jazz and ten years down the line has set up another group. Throughout the Tarot runs the theme of choice and we can never predict what might have been, had we chosen otherwise. But at any point we can pick up promising strands that we did not develop.

Jean's Judgement was revealed when she contacted her birth family. Her adoptive mother had been very upset by the idea so Jean had not met her birth mother who had died 12 years before. With the recent death of her adoptive mother, Jean felt that it was at last the right time to learn about her past and to put behind her the guilt and regrets about refusing to meet her natural mother.

The negative aspect of Judgement is best summed up in the phrase 'against your better judgement' when logic and common sense are warning you not to rush ahead blindly. When this meaning appears, then you will know it's time to listen to your head and not your heart.

The World

The final card in the Major Arcana does look to the future, but in a positive way, representing the state of equilibrium that can be attained by stepping off the relentless Wheel of Time. It is the card of the Holy Grail, the end of the Quest and yet at the same time, in a sense, it is really the beginning, for the Fool is seen in many World cards as the dancer at the still point of the turning world or wheel, surrounded by greenery and with symbols of the four elements in the corners.

THE WORLD.

The Fool's journey represents the search we all make for spiritual evolution, in essence a voyage of self-discovery, for we all possess the cosmic or divine spark within us.

This truly is the card of the wise counsellor for, whatever age you are, you possess mature balanced judgement and are comfortable within your skin, not afraid to look in the mirror or to walk into a crowded room alone. For you recognise, and others see in you, the inner radiance that is the most effective makeover in the world.

The World is primarily a card of movement and going forward, whether this involves actual travel or being open to new perspectives and ideas. Or it may be a sense of rightness, that your life is on course and that the pieces are falling into shape. For, however, far you travel, you are still yourself and carry your home within. Much as you love those around you, there are times when you are happy to be yourself and by yourself. You know now that being alone is not the same as being lonely and so, ironically, as you come to depend on people less for your emotional fulfilment, real closeness is more possible.

It's hard to find a negative side of the World card, but sometimes we are swept along by events and so involved in activity that we may feel that we are losing touch with the people who matter to us. Others may find it hard to accept change and we may need to be patient if we want to take our loved ones with us.

A reading of nine cards

This follows exactly the same pattern as for three- and six-card readings and is to me the most useful format for major readings in my own life or for others, especially if I have not met the person before. You will find that as the cards are added, so the picture builds up, so if a card is unclear, leave its interpretation until other cards have created the context.

Deal from left to right, with the first row nearest to you, and then right to left for the middle row and left to right for the top row. A questioner should lay out the cards in the same order, so that the first row is nearest and facing him or her.

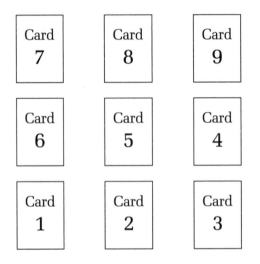

It is easier to turn over all nine cards before beginning the reading and then the card order will become intuitively clear.

Rachel's reading of nine

The question seems very straightforward – whether Rachel should sell her house and move into her new partner Richard's much larger house, thus saving paying one mortgage. Rachel, now in her late thirties, has lived in her own home for more than ten years. But much as she loves Richard, whom she has been seeing regularly for five years, she likes her own space and fears that she is too set in her ways to change. What is more, Richard works overnight shifts as a driver and she finds it difficult to adjust to the different sleep patterns. Richard has never shared a house since he left home in his mid-twenties.

Using the Major Arcana, Rachael picks the following nine cards:

Card 1 Death

Card 2 The Hierophant

Card 3 Judgement

Card 4 The Magician

Card 5 The High Priestess

Card 6 The Tower

Card 7 The Hermit

Card 8 The Chariot

Card 9 The World

Rachel reads the first six cards in the order they were dealt, but leaves the Hermit to the end.

Death

A strange card for the beginning of a new permanent phase in the relationship, but there is still a lot Rachel needs to resolve. She says she feels that it will be almost a bereavement to leave the home she loves so much, though she accepts it is not practical for Richard to move into her house, as it is so small.

The Hierophant

This is a card of tradition and the conventional path. Rachel interprets it as the formalisation of a relationship that has continued for almost five years. How does Rachel feel about this? She says that she is being pressurised by Richard's family to move in with him, they hope as a prelude to a wedding, as they are a very close-knit, conventional family. But she would prefer to keep her own space as she feels that she is being taken over, especially when Richard's large family visit his home.

Judgement

Rachel said that she felt guilty because she was so reluctant to sell her house, as it made sense economically not to run two places and that she and Richard had a very loving relationship. She would feel equally reluctant if Richard was selling his home to move with her, as she and Richard had very different lifestyles. Richard was the domesticated, tidy one with a well-tended garden, while she lived in organised chaos, painting in her spare time, and her sink was as likely to be filled with her watercolour pots as with dishes in which she had made delicious casseroles. She always felt on her best behaviour at Richard's house and he was constantly clearing up after her. So Judgement here is about different criteria and questions whether Rachel could or should adapt to Richard's world and if he too can accept a more relaxed home life if he moves in.

The Magician

Rachel was reminded that Richard had told her many times that she brought magic and vitality into his world.

But what inspirational solution lies in this card? Recently, she had been wondering whether they should buy a different joint home, so that neither had to give up territorial rights entirely and they could establish a mutually acceptable way of living together in new surroundings. If this was a larger place, then each could have some personal space, in Rachel's case for her painting materials and canvases. They might not save much money as the mortgage, would be higher, but it would be an investment. A larger garden would also allow Rachel to create a wilderness area without encroaching on Richard's more formal garden.

The High Priestess

Both Rachel and Richard were very private people and over the years they had become set in their ways. Were it not for the expectations of friends and family, Rachel admitted that they would probably continue in their present relationship, which allowed them the benefits of marriage, but the freedom to be alone when they wished. Neither had been seriously involved with other people before, as Rachel had taken care of her young brothers and sisters for several years after her mother died. So in a sense she had exhausted her nurturing family instincts, while Richard, who had spent several years crewing yachts, hated the camaraderie and chaos of his large family. Each saw in the other the oasis of calm they needed.

The Tower

From the above, it seems that all could be left as it was; but the Tower suggested the need to break free from stagnation and sterility. Rachel admitted that she and Richard had agreed that they needed either to make a commitment to each other in the near future or to part, as their relationship, although perfect in many ways, was not progressing. So the house move, though prompted by Richard's family, represented a major step that in her heart Rachel knew was necessary if the relationship was to evolve.

The Chariot

This card indicates a change of direction and Rachel said that she and Richard had vaguely talked about setting up in business together. She taught art at the local secondary school, but had for years wanted to teach painting to adults. Richard had suggested they opened a holiday centre in the Lake District where she could teach painting to guests and he could organise tours of the area and teach sailing. Could this be the time to invest their money as a deposit on a guest house? It would be a financial risk, but both had substantial savings.

The World

This augured travel and movement and promises harmony and a sense of integration, if Rachel widened her horizons, both mentally and physically and explored the possibilities that are at this change point open to her. Rachel decided they should explore some of the options before deciding on a future, since they were both still relatively young and in a sense had opted out of both commitment and of developing their potential. Rachel especially has become increasingly frustrated over recent months with her teaching post, which was restricted by government guidelines and examinations (another Tower reference).

The Hermit

It might have seemed more natural to have the World as the last card. But the Hermit talks about creative withdrawal and this, Rachel felt, referred to the influence of Richard's family who were trying to force them into settling down in what they saw as the right mode of living. But the significance of the Hermit went deeper. Though she had withdrawn emotionally after so many years of caring for her brothers and sisters and her father, Rachel needed now to allow herself time and to talk to Richard about her buried negative feelings. She had never come to terms with her mother's death, which had left her responsible for her family with a father who left all the problems for Rachel to resolve while he went out every night. Only then would Rachel be ready to move forward into what could be a fulfilling life in every way.

The Minor Arcana

⁜

Some people read only the Major Arcana, believing that the Minor Cards are too detailed and limited in scope to allow intuition to flow, as it does with the archetypal cards. However, for others the Minor Arcana makes a reading more focused by specifically pinpointing areas and strategies. The four Tarot suits have a great deal of symbolism attached. Each represents one of the four elemental forces but, with the growth of the modern Western magical tradition, the Tarot suits have also become associated with the four Celtic Treasures and the Christian Treasures of the Holy Grail.

The Celtic Treasures

Earth: Pentacles (discs/coins)
The original symbol, the *Lia Fail* stone, once stood on Tara, the Hill of the Tuaatha–Danaan, the ancient Irish hero–gods. It was the stone on which the High Kings of Ireland were crowned and was said to emit a high-pitched cry when a true king stood upon it. It was later taken to Scotland as the Stone of Scone, and was moved from there to England by Edward I in 1297 and placed under the Coronation throne in Westminster Abbey. It has now been restored to Scotland.

Air: Swords
This is the Sword of Nuada of the Silver Hand, whose sword hand was cut off in battle. With a new hand fashioned of silver, he went on to lead his people to victory. It is also associated with Lugh, the hero who became the young Celtic Sun God. Like the other Celtic

elemental symbols it was one of the treasures of the Dagda, the Father God.

In myth, to take up the invincible Sword of Light that blazed with flame in battle, except in dire need, would bring death to the user.

Fire: Wands (spears/batons/staves)
The spear, Birgha, originally belonged to Lugh, who used it to slay his own grandfather, the old solar god Balor, and so brought about the new order. Like other magical spears in mythology, Birgha always hit its target and returned to the hand of the owner. It created fire when it was thrown in a noble cause.

Water: Cups (chalices)
The most fascinating of the great treasures is known as the Cauldron of Plenty or the Undry that provided an endless supply of nourishment, had great healing powers and could revive the dead, either to their former existence or a new life form. The Cauldron could also be accessed by magical means or spiritual quests by the living and was located on the Isle of Arran, one of the Celtic Isles of the Blest.

The Christian Treasures

These Grail treasures were believed by the fifth-century Greek historian, Olympiadorus, to have been brought to Britain for safety when Rome was sacked by the Visigoths, possibly passing to Arthur at his stronghold near Shrewsbury for safe keeping in a specially erected chapel. However, other tradition says that Joseph of Arimathea brought them to Glastonbury in 64 AD.

Pentacles symbolise the dish from which Jesus ate the paschal lamb and is sometimes said to be the original Holy Grail.

Swords symbolise the Sword of King David.

Wands symbolise the sacred lance that pierced Jesus's side.

Cups symbolise the chalice that Christ used at the Last Supper, in which His blood was collected after the crucifixion. There is the possibility that there were two Grail cups, one owned by Mary Magdalene and one by Joseph of Arimathea, the wealthy merchant who cared for Christ's body after death.

The meanings of the suits in divination

We met the four elements when consecrating the Tarot pack and creating a circle of power and protection. Plato, the Greek philosopher who lived around 360 BC, recounted in his book *Timaeus* that Demiurge, the god of creation, made the world out of the four elements: Earth, Air, Fire and Water. This world included the earth and the celestial sphere of moon, stars and sun. Humankind was therefore made up of the four elements in different proportions, which explained the predominant character types observed first by the Greeks. This tradition continued through Roman times to the Middle Ages and Tudor times.

In our own age, the psychologist Carl Gustav Jung identified the four elements with four basic ways of functioning: Earth with sensations; Air with thinking; Fire with intuition and Water with feeling. This has greatly influenced modern Tarot reading and so without knowing the specific meanings of each Number Card, you can apply your intuitive approach as well as what you know about each suit to clarify the meanings in readings.

Pentacles – woman at home
Earth is the element of order, both in nature and in institutions such as the law, politics, finance, health and education. It represents the female, yin, nurturing, goddess aspect, Mother Earth, the home and family as well as money and security.

Pentacles correspond to the element of Earth and are the nuts and bolts that hold the practical world together. Women are usually good at making things happen, as opposed to some men whose cave-building instincts are exhausted just by buying a forest of ready-sanded timber and a collection of state-of-the-art tools to clutter up the patio.

Pentacles are traditionally linked with money and so, when they predominate in a reading, financial matters may predominate, whether these are money-making schemes, a reordering of finances or delicate negotiations on financial matters. Some women still find that if they do give up paid work for a time or cut down, perhaps to care for a young child, the ever-open cash-box of the carefree days before children arrived suddenly has a lock and key. A high-earning woman in a partnership can equally seem a threat to the paper-thin ego of an insecure male, especially if he works as house-husband. But also under the auspices of Pentacles are all domestic and family matters, home and issues of security and property, everyday practicalities of life, physical and material security, property, legal and official matters, children and animals. When Pentacles appear, they give assurance that any plan has firm foundations for any venture.

Swords – woman and the world

Air represents life itself, logic, the mind, courage and focus, the male, yang god in the form of sky deities. Swords correspond to the element of Air and are the suit of logic and determination. They speak of limitations and obstacles but also of the power to initiate change, especially under difficult circumstances. Swords may not seem particularly female-friendly, but the power of the sword may be needed when a situation seems unjust – they frequently appear with the Justice cards in readings. What is more, even in the sunniest reading, a Sword or two ensures that your mind is checking out the small print of happiness, which, like Pentacles, translates dreams into reality – and still leaves you with the taxi fare home.

Swords are the suit of courage, tradition, the conventional path, formal learning, formal and informal justice and assessment, older people and ageing. When they appear, it is a time for the head, not the heart, to rule and to be single-minded, using the sword to cut through indecision and inertia and ride forth to victory.

Wands – independent woman

Fire represents light, the Sun, lightning, fertility, power, joy, ambition, inspiration and achievement and also destruction of what is now no longer needed. Like Air, it is the male, yang, god in the form of the Sun deities, exuding creativity, originality and individuality. But as we saw with the Sun card there are plenty of female solar deities also brimming with golden animus power and so this is woman at her most dynamic, whatever her age or lifestyle.

The Wands are the most exciting suit for personal ventures and creativity that comes from within you and they concern your personal happiness. Wands indicate spontaneity and joy and may be a suit that more traditional men find hard to cope with in women.

For the Wands are the suit of beginnings, the world of ideas and ideals, of energy, career, travel, health and above all action. When they appear, it is a time to believe in yourself and to follow your dreams in your personal or work sphere, as you ride your personal rocket to the stars.

Cups – woman of love
Water represents love, relationships, sympathy, intuition, healing and the cycle of birth, death and rebirth. Like Earth, it represents the female, yin goddess in the form of the Moon.

Cups are linked to the element Water and also with our emotional life, our feelings and the relationships that are so vital to our happiness. They may indicate a commitment of the heart in the offing or some hidden or unacknowledged turmoil in our relationships with family, close friends and colleagues. They refer also to issues of fertility, healing, peace and reconciliation with others, sensitivity, adaptability and gentleness and the world of dreams and psychic awareness, to people in their twenties and thirties and all who are in love, whatever their age.

When Cups appear, you should do what you feel and not what you think is right and above all follow your heart and, like water, go with the flow. Tune into what people mean, which may be very different from what they say and do.

DAY 12
The Aces

✛

As the Minor Arcana is very detailed, I would suggest that during this period, you concentrate on using the basic unstructured three, six and nine formats, while you assimilate the card meanings. After the Tens, I will introduce another basic spread and later in the book I will give other more complex layouts that I have found useful.

Aces are especially good cards to find in a reading. Ruled by the Sun, they indicate not only new beginnings, but the inflow of energy and enthusiasm into your life. You can tell the area to which the Ace refers by its ruling suit, but if there is more than one Ace, you will feel the stirrings of hope permeate every aspect of your being.

You may be offered a new opportunity, experience a sudden change of plan or perspective or just wake up and find the sun is shining after all; confidence returns, along with new ideas and ingenious solutions to long-standing problems. Although at the beginning of this section, I described the four suits in their elemental order, in divination they are generally arranged in the sequence in which I have introduced them below. However, it makes no practical difference except in the order of learning.

The elemental order is used in Tarot spells and rituals, such as those described on Day 29, Magic and Psychic Awareness (see pages 173–84).

The Ace of Pentacles

ACE of PENTACLES

This Ace promises a new beginning in a practical or material way, whether it is a desire or opportunity to change your job or home or to learn a new skill to adapt to the changing world. Many opportunities do occur because we are open to possibilities and see new avenues that might have passed us by in a more introspective mood.

Being Pentacles, it indicates that you will not cover great distances in the first hours or even days of your new beginning but, because you are well prepared, you will not be deterred when you meet the first obstacle. You may also become involved in a new home-related project or an upsurge in prosperity.

The only negative aspect is when you take on a new practical or financial responsibility that is for the benefit of others that may drain your resources and energy.

The Ace of Cups

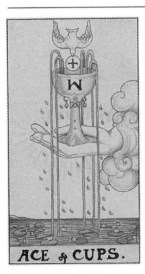

ACE of CUPS.

The Ace of Cups is a card of joy, representing a new beginning emotionally, whether a new relationship or friendship, a new stage in a relationship or indeed the beginning of a more spiritual path; it can also indicate the stirrings of trust after betrayal, or a new start after an emotional setback or broken relationship, or the conception or birth of a baby.

Of course we all experience many new beginnings that can be as poignantly sweet as first love, whatever our age or experience, and as women move from one phase to another there are many times when we may feel uncertain, as we leave behind our emotional certainty or stagnation and reach out to another person.

How can this card be negative? Only if we begin expecting perfection and endow so much emotion to the beginning of the relationship that it cannot be sustained.

The Ace of Wands

The most dynamic number combined with the most energising suit makes this a very magical Wand, still budding with life. So how can you doubt any plan you wish to put into practice, any quest for personal joy, any new idea, new spiritual or divinatory technique or place to visit whose call cannot be ignored?

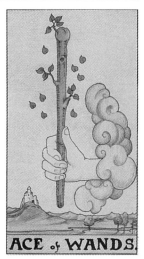

This is the Ace of new beginnings in career, a quest for promotion, an unexpected opportunity to travel or to learn something new and creative, improved health or even an awareness that you desire freedom from a restricting situation. Whether you want to write poetry, paint, get a job in radio or television, patent your new invention or just rejoice in being alive, today is the time to make it happen.

This Ace could only be negative if you have a trail of new beginnings that never get beyond first base.

The Ace of Swords

So maybe this new beginning was not the heroine's send-off inherent in the last card? Maybe you have got to build your rocket from the DIY 'try again' kit. This card can herald a beginning under difficult circumstances, maybe after a business failure or a broken relationship, or just a lot of small but pervasive setbacks or critical, demanding people who have drained you of enthusiasm.

ACE ₒᵧ SWORDS.

But if you have used your heart too much in the past and been held back by those who have played upon your sentiments, now is a chance to use your head and incisive logic, for this is a powerful, positive card of change, whether this is on a personal or professional level, and obstacles become a catalyst for new directions.

You are wise and experienced and so will appreciate all the good things that will result from this beginning, even if it was not the route you might have chosen. Only if you defeat yourself before you begin by listening to the redundant and superfluous voices of yesterday could this card be negative.

The Twos

✛

Two is ruled by the waxing moon and though the energies are consequently less focused than that of the Aces, these can be very positive cards, promising gentle growth whether in love or opportunity. They deal with partnership issues, both in love and business, and with balancing events or resolving disparate demands on our time. And like the moon, the balance can ebb and flow so that sometimes it may feel as if we are trying to juggle two balls that keep flying in opposite directions. At other times, we may experience the harmony of two people dancing in step.

And so in a reading the Twos can be a number of harmony or division, of double the strength or the splitting of power and resources in opposite directions. Duality is a key concept in the Tarot and a woman's life, in which she is constantly balancing her nurturing and independent sides, her assertive drive with the receptive inner world, thought and feeling, conscious and unconscious wisdom, practical and spiritual calls on time and energy – and of course of different people who may demand you mediate or choose between them. As you work with your psychic powers, so this process of integration will become more natural and involve less conscious effort, and the conflicts affect your own harmony less and less.

The Two of Pentacles

This card represents for many women the ongoing struggle to give enough time to both work and home or family commitments, the mental and physical demands on time and also the need for spiritual space to evolve and withdraw from the frantic world. But it does have positive connotations, indicating that you may be

developing in two different directions, perhaps an interest that could turn into an alternative career or a relationship that right now means you have less time to spend with friends – in such cases the balance will right itself. It may also indicate a recent or potential partnership to forward mutual interests or even a extra source of income that may be on the horizon.

The negative aspect comes if you are feeling exhausted and never have a moment to yourself. As the current psycho-jargon tells us, 'prioritise and delegate', even to those who are unwilling to do their share.

The Two of Cups

This is a card that will lift any reading, for it may herald the deepening of a relationship, whether love or friendship, the mending of a quarrel or a period of emotional harmony, even a firm commitment of love or marriage.

But it can equally refer to the integration of two aspects of your life, perhaps your home and work life or your intellectual and spiritual sides that both have a place and can mutually enrich the other. Perhaps it is an indicator that you and a loved one need more time together to strengthen or rekindle your relationship or even that you need to confide in a friend if you have been feeling lonely.

Only when choices are demanded, between two family members or between a partner and parent, partner and child or in a work dispute, does this card become negative – resist the temptation to be drawn into the quarrels of others or in making choices others have no right to demand of you.

The Two of Wands

This is the card of alternatives and is unusually static for Wands; it suggests that if there are two paths or options before you or a general restlessness, you should wait and use your inspirational powers for thought and forward planning, so that you can be certain you are taking the right course.

This card may appear when the right option or opportunity has not turned up; but it will if you can be patient. You may feel that in some area you want to strike out alone or try something new, but if you do move on, try to identify where you are going rather than just pressing ahead blindly. Plans involving others may seem temporarily restrictive and business partnerships or work relationships may need revitalising or renegotiating. You do not want to settle for second-best, so let the cosmos catch up with you before making a decision.

The negative aspect may be reflected in a sense of malaise or minor ill-health that may indicate you have been trying to cram too much into your life, with the result that your normal enthusiasm for life is diluted – go with your energy flows and listen to your body as well as your mind, which may be telling you to slow down.

The Two of Swords

In this card, it is the negative aspect of the Swords that is to the fore, the fears that freeze you into inaction. Clearly you have choices, none of which may be ideal, and perhaps pressure from others to follow one particular path. Perhaps significantly, these 'fear' cards do in many packs portray a woman who is afraid to choose. This does not indicate that women have less courage than men, but that they have often a deeper awareness of the consequences of actions.

This awareness is apparent in the many women who have stayed in an unhappy situation because they know what hurt or damage would be caused to others who depend on them if there were a break-up. For example, far fewer women than men will walk out of a relationship, leaving children behind, or will quit a no-win job situation over a matter of principle if they know their earnings are vital to maintain the home.

It is for this reason that some mothers, single ones especially, accept quite unfair treatment; it is not because they are weak or stupid, but because during the time it takes for a case to reach court, they will have no money.

Whatever the situation, it is a time to use your head and to face courageously the choices, which may involve declining both options; and therein lies the positive aspect of this card.

The Threes

✛

Three is the number of increase, as two combine to become three, for example in alchemy where King Sol and Queen Luna (the symbols of One and Two) have produced the Divine Child that is greater than them. Threes, ruled by the expansive Jupiter, may indicate an increase in joy, an addition to a family circle, group of friends, an additional employee or colleague who will have a positive effect and also the need for extra input whether in a relationship or at work. As a short-term outcome of actions or decisions suggested by a reading, any Three card in a reading augurs the achievement of initial goals in the area to which the suit points. Above all, Threes indicate that co-operation is the best way to achieve results, so it is a time for family or corporate action, rather than striking out alone.

The Three of Pentacles

Working with others, pooling either resources, talents or finances, would be a constructive approach in most situations. You may be due to receive some financial reward or tangible recognition for earlier investment or effort. If you are doubting whether your input into the home and family is worthwhile, you will see in the very near future an upward trend in affairs and real, if modest, results taking shape.

Because others do feel at home with you, you may acquire extra house guests. A traditional meaning for this card, like that of the Three of Cups, is that it heralds a pregnancy, birth or addition to the family or immediate circle of friends; with Pentacles, however, such an addition is often the result of acquiring relatives through a new marriage or liaison, not necessarily your own, or an elderly or sick relative or friend, rather than an infant who needs some temporary attention. However, any extra commitments or responsibilities will prove to be of long-term advantage.

The negative aspect of this card appears when you take on extra practical burdens out of a sense of duty that may weigh heavy at a time when you are already over-committed – if so, consider delegating or getting external help.

The Three of Cups

This card shows an abundance of flowers and wine and depicts two people celebrating the addition of a third, a newcomer.

The third person may be literally taken as meaning a new baby, but may equally refer to any kind of special occasion or gathering of family or friends. So it indicates that you may acquire new friends or a join a group that brings you joy and emotional satisfaction; an absent friend or family member may return, for, like the Two of Cups, this is a card of reconciliation. But it can also indicate a child returning to the nest or simply a period of emotional happiness in the family, perhaps after prolonged turbulence.

Above all, the Three of Cups is a reminder to enjoy the friendship and love of those who are close to you, for goodwill that you build up now will return threefold later. Extend an olive branch to estranged family members or friends – men especially can bear grudges for years over trivial slights. But your tact and ability to make others welcome can mend fences at this time.

Only when there is longstanding underlying jealousy or animosity among family or friends can this card be problematic, so lay down ground rules for abiding by a truce, or avoid inviting persistent trouble-makers.

The Three of Wands

There has been progress from the Two of Wands and natural energies are flowing again.

Being a card of communication, it indicates a time for networking and contacting useful sources at and through work, applying for or continuing with courses and for formulating short-term plans. The future is very open, but any stagnation is clearing and you are, or will be, entering a period of movement, either mental or actual. The more effort you put into bringing plans to fruition and the further you explore, the wider your horizons and future options will be. You have everything to play for.

The negative aspect may be a growing realisation that growth and movement may involve leaving safe familiar work practices behind or to the need to express views that may differ from those who see less clearly.

The Three of Swords

This can on the surface seem a very gloomy card, depicting rain, storm clouds or a pierced heart, and the negative and positive aspects are closely interwoven, as with other Sword cards. But because Tarot images are symbolic, rather than literal, logic is, in fact, triumphing over sentiment or perhaps emotional blackmail, gossip and spite, probably from a small group of people who resent your abilities. The Three of Swords can also indicate that

you are being too receptive to the hard-luck stories of others. Women are naturally soft-hearted but colleagues, employees, friends and even strangers can home in on a soft target and leave you laden with extra work and responsibility – and less well off.

If, however, you have been feeling emotionally vulnerable, now is not the time to show weakness, except to those close to you, but to assume the mask of reason. Weakness or appeals to the better nature of others will not be effective, so use strength in the world outside your front door to get what you need – and deserve.

DAY 15

The Fours

✛

The Fours are ruled by the Evening Sun and are cards of organisation and stability or limitation, depending on both the suit and the interpretation you give to the card. They are in fact the 'reality principle', where ideas, plans and even relationships must be adapted to the world as it is, not the world we should like it to be.

But that is not to say that we cannot widen the horizons of that existing reality and sometimes it is important to step into the unknown rather than hold ourselves back where we know it is safe. Many of the limitations we impose on our lives derive from our fear of change and the unknown.

As I have said many times in this book, women now have opportunities undreamed-of 50 or even 20 years ago. Yet they have always faced challenges; think of early mediaeval women mystics like Hildegard von Bingen who challenged popes, bishops and nobles at a time when the opinion of a woman meant nothing. Suffragettes were imprisoned for demanding political equality and early feminists paved the way for fairer legislation on both sides of the Atlantic; missionaries and philanthropists such as Mother Teresa of Calcutta have lived in appalling conditions caring for people cast away in the gutter. But the fears have always been there, and still are, whether a woman takes a job as an astronaut, drives convoy lorries to Bosnia, determines to live her life alone, gives birth to another human and nurtures him or her for 20 years or more, or turns her back on fate and fortune for a cause she considers worthwhile.

The Four of Pentacles

'Be content with what you have' is a maxim fed to us with our mothers' milk. This is the card of holding on to what has been attained in a practical or material sense.

We may be afraid of losing what we have if we do embark on a new course of action, whether moving or leaving home, working from home in a self-employed capacity, investing money in a project or a course that may bring spiritual rather than tangible rewards, or turning our back on a safe option to explore pastures new. This card may appear in a reading with the Four of Cups, for strong emotions are often evoked by practical choices involving risk, especially connected with the domestic world.

But there is another saying, 'To speculate is to accumulate', and what you may lose in material wealth or domestic certainty, you – and your loved ones – may gain in a more fulfilling way of life.

The only negative aspect comes if those close to you are jeopardising your future by their foolhardiness – it may be necessary to reduce or cut off your source of support.

The Four of Cups

This is sometimes called the card of divine discontent, because what is being offered in actual relationships or emotional fulfilment is not enough. And there lies the inbuilt aspect of this card: a free-floating desire for something more exciting that puts at risk a worthwhile existing relationship or friendship.

But the card can represent any relationship, friendship or situation where emotions are involved and you need to decide whether to develop that relationship further, perhaps whether to trust or commit or whether to hold back. Equally, you may be feeling pressurised by the emotions or emotional demands of

others, especially if you are being persuaded to stay in a situation or relationship against your better judgement, or to offer promises you are not certain you can or wish to keep. Women can sometimes allow ex-partners or friends to manipulate their heart-strings and so hold themselves back from moving on.

General feelings of restlessness and emotional dissatisfaction sometimes mean you need to make changes in an existing relationship, especially if you are feeling stifled, or it may be that your own or another person's commitment is under question. Acknowledge any doubts and if possible talk them through with a trusted friend or the person concerned. If you are alone or have been hurt, you may have a growing realisation that it is time to allow your emotional side to emerge once more and to widen your social circle.

The Four of Wands

This is the most positive of the Four cards and is rooted in the reality principle of what has been or will soon be achieved here and now. In the past, I have perhaps not appreciated how important this card is in affirming that ideas, career ambitions and personal fulfilment can be attained within the context of your present world.

This is also a very predictive card, promising success if you use your originality and drive to make improvements in existing working practices and within yourself, perhaps through new interests, a deeper study of spirituality or just enjoying what you have and who you are. It is a very stable card, which recognises that it is important to develop your self as well as your career and to make time for friends and family. It epitomises the ideal or the core of the Tarot for women, the realisation that spirituality and magic really can happen in those few minutes you may have for yourself in the hurly-burly of your day.

The only danger is if the security aspect does become imprisoning and you do not move on to fulfil your ultimate goal.

The Four of Swords

This is the second Swords card in which the negative aspect is the focus of the card, but it is not a real danger or fear that holds you in its thrall. Being a Four, the fear is of loss of security, probably the approval of others.

But much of that approval you are seeking may be from the voices of the past and these can be far more discouraging than any current opposition to your plans. Women with their richly creative imaginations can revive those old ghosts all too vividly, the voice of your mother or grandmother telling you that you would never be as clever as your brother or as pretty as your sister. Maybe she acted out of the best motives or spoke from her own disappointment, like the teacher who could not bear to praise you or admit you might be more talented than she was. You may still hesitate from giving yourself fully in love-making, because an ex told you that you were frigid when you refused to indulge in casual sex or did not want him videotaping you in bed and playing the results at the rugby club annual dinner. A woman with a truly beautiful figure may hide it under baggy clothes because some malicious, envious friend said she was fat.

So this card tells you to go for whatever you want with confidence and shed the distorted doubts that may be holding you back.

DAY 16
The Fives

✛

The Fives are said to be ruled by the planet Mercury and so are linked with both communication and versatility. The traditional instability of the Tarot Fives reflects this quicksilver quality and so they are invariably cards of change, the catalyst for reassessment of areas of life that seem stagnant. They can have very positive meanings, for the communication of personal needs, dreams and worries to those around us can lead to more meaningful work and personal relationships. But Mercury also has a strongly challenging trickster element, so there may be some confusion or even malice by others, to which the Fives act as an early-warning system, thus allowing clear communication to bring light to shadowy areas of life.

The Five of Pentacles

This card may reflect unvoiced worries about a financial or domestic matter, perhaps a temporary cash-flow problem, a hiccup in the organisation of your life or the behaviour of a member of the family or a close friend whose problems are weighing heavily on you. Strong, independent women tend to act as a mobile resource centre for the world. So when they feel vulnerable, others may not recognise this need.

The Five of Pentacles can also appear if you are feeling isolated from family or friends, either physically or because of a financial or domestic disagreement. If you live or work alone, you may benefit from support or friendship beyond your immediate environment. My Swedish e-mail friend Susanne is a lifeline to me during many a late-night solitary session on my computer, as she too burns the midnight oil with her work.

The negative aspect of the card is that friends, family and colleagues may be so unreceptive or preoccupied with their own lives, that you may need to seek support from a new source, maybe someone you might not have thought of as particularly friendly or understanding, or an organisation that has the resources, if not to solve the problem, then to point you in the right direction.

The Five of Cups

The Five of Cups has negative connotations within its general meaning, representing undue focus on what has been lost or not fulfilled emotionally, rather than what still exists and has potential for fruition.

It may be a card of negative perspective and may instigate a desire to walk away from, rather then resolve, an emotional situation that may have hit a difficult or mundane period. Suddenly, the person on the train you see every morning or the new sales representative with the gleaming smile and matching car may become far more attractive. Conversely, your partner may suddenly start applying aftershave to normally inaccessible parts of their anatomy or staying away overnight when they normally consider catching the 19.15 train as a late night out.

Maybe you feel friends or colleagues are taking you for granted or adult children using you as a late-night grocery store and a babysitting service for grandchildren. In any situation, it may be tempting to buy a bar in Spain or try a new model. But, as my late mother always said, the grass may be greener on the other side of the fence, but it may also have been sprayed with pesticide – or worse. So communicate with the source of your dissatisfaction or boredom and be prepared to accept that you may bear some responsibility for the impasse. For once, listening to other people rather than your heart may give the best advice.

The Five of Wands

The Five of Wands reflects the less honourable aspects of Mercury and you may need to fight your corner, especially in the outside and workaday worlds.

You should be certain to get full credit for your input and, while you may have to fight for your ideal and ideas, this is not a time to compromise over principles. If you make any communication, either verbal or written, make it unambiguous and focused, rather than emotive, to ensure you have every chance of success. Even if you are taking on a large organisation, or seeking independence from one, you should continue to believe in yourself – remember David's success against the giant Goliath.

On the negative side, you may feel tired and take less care of yourself than usual, which can result in minor accidents and stress-related illnesses. So it is a time to put *yourself* very near the top of your personal priorities.

The Five of Swords

The Five of Swords is another card for fighting your corner, but you may find that it is the more subtle approach of the Swords – reason, logic and certainly your facts and figures – that will enable you to win through. You may have been subjected to unfair gossip

or criticism, to bullying tactics or undeserved hostility from others. If this attack has come from people you trusted or cared for, it may have wounded you.

Or you may feel temporarily overwhelmed by the odds against you, perhaps by officialdom or by the sheer volume of letters, faxes or e-mails you need to send and the background material you have to master in order to put your point clearly and concisely. This card has close links with the previous one and they may appear together when work or official matters loom large.

The negative aspect says that you should be aware that others may be less than honest in their dealings – after all, Mercury is also associated with moneylenders and thieves. You may need to be less open about your intentions.

The Sixes

✛

The Sixes are in contrast a stable number, ruled by Venus, the goddess of love and the Morning Star. Consequently, they reflect harmony, especially in matters close to the heart. However, Venus also brings an element of escapism and in her guise as a warrior goddess she is quite a feisty lady, thus counteracting tendencies towards marshmallow sentimentality.

So the Sixes reflect an idealised state of peace, equality and fairness in every area of life. Sometimes, however, the reality does not live up to the expectations, thus requiring either a movement towards a more harmonious state of affairs or demisting the rose-tinted spectacles that can prevent us from maximising the advantages of our present situation.

The Six of Pentacles

This card is a natural expression of the abundance and generosity inherent in all cards ruled by Venus. Your support is important to loved ones and you derive great pleasure from creating a welcoming home and giving time – or money – to those around you.

But it is important to identify yourself as the giver in the card, so that that the balance is maintained between giving and accepting from others. This is a concept that some women, myself included, find difficult, and as I struggle to maintain my

Little Mother Courage role in personal as well as working situations, I am aware that sometimes I am very bad at accepting help, gifts or, above all, praise. It is also necessary to give to *yourself* the time and encouragement you offer to others.

The negative aspect is that if you do give indiscriminately to others, you may not only find that you end up with nothing left to give to those you do love most, but also that you may lock others in a dependency relationship that is mutually destructive.

The Six of Cups

The Six of Cups really is the card of rose-tinted spectacles, first love, heady days of freedom or even those early stages of a relationship when the sun shone every day and his mother wore the good fairy's crown and not the witch's hat.

Such retouched memories can be of value in rekindling earlier feelings and enthusiasms that may have become buried in the demands of the everyday world. This applies just as much to our personal feelings, which get blunted so that we may no longer enjoy the anticipation of each new day. When this card appears, you may need to spend more time developing your personal world and getting back in touch with your true feelings. Even a day or two away, especially in places that hold happy memories for you, can revive your natural optimism and do wonders for a relationship that has hit a plateau.

Contacting old friends and perhaps rekindling friendships that have faded, through lack of time rather than loss of affection, may help you to centre yourself and make contact with your roots, for above all, this is the card of you from the earliest days of your childhood to your old age when you will be the archetypal Wise Woman – the essential core person that makes you unique.

Only if you try to turn the clock back to a stage of your life that no longer exists or to relationships best dead and buried can this card have negative connotations.

The Six of Wands

This is the Six card at its most positive, assuring you that the path you are on or intend to follow is the right one and will bring success and recognition, even from those who doubted you.

More important, however, it represents an inner confidence and a certainty that you have within you the ability, whatever your age or stage of life, to integrate all the disparate elements of your life; it confirms the knowledge that you do not need, though you may value, the approval of others. So whether it concerns a personal dream or life plan, short-term goal, creative or spiritual enterprise, your hard work and the setbacks you have overcome have been worthwhile – so stay on course.

This card does not have a negative side, unless you sacrifice your harmony to fulfil the dreams others have set for you, a recurring theme of the Tarot.

The Six of Swords

Here even the turbulent Swords promise a period of harmony. The Six of Swords says that calmer times are ahead, perhaps after unrest or uncertainty.

This card is sometimes taken to indicate travel, often a well-deserved holiday or short break, and if you do not have one planned, then even a short period away from sad memories or ongoing problems will restore inner harmony and may replace negative feelings with the good memories of the Six of Cups, this

card's alter-ego. You may also be contemplating a house-move, perhaps for a fresh start or to find a place with which you feel more in tune than your present location.

If you are dealt the Six of Swords, it may also indicate a psychic movement to a new level of spiritual evolution, perhaps connection with your inner stillness through meditation or quiet contemplation by candlelight or moonlight. Though Swords do talk of logic, this is a time to move beyond the conscious rational mind and you may discover psychic abilities that have lain dormant and unrecognised in you since childhood.

The only negative aspect is if you carry with you regrets or bitterness for past injustices done to you or old losses that cannot be compensated.

DAY 18
The Sevens

✥

The Sevens are ruled by the waning moon and so the energies are those of the inner world and the mysterious face of the Moon, mistress of the psyche and of unconscious wisdom. Seven is the most spiritual and mysterious number and so these cards are concerned with spiritual awareness rather than achievement or material success. This is the questioning quartet. Time to answer the underlying questions about the purpose and meaning of our lives is sometimes pushed aside in the modern world. The down-rush of energy that leaves us temporarily stranded on the shore may be alleviated by a quick sugar fix or stimulating music or activity, rather than used for contemplation and introspection. So take time, when your Sevens appear, to sit a while with your reading and let the insights flow.

The Seven of Pentacles

The Seven of Pentacles is the card of the harvest, a natural time to pause and assess what has gone before and what is to come. The task before you may need re-examining or you may have reached a point when you are assessing what it is you are working for and if this is the best way to continue.

All very contemplative for a Pentacles card. Long-term material security is augured, but perhaps the sheer effort of living has blocked out another important side of you – and the joy of living. Do you need a different kind of home, or have circumstances changed so that you should modify your domestic arrangements? For example, those baby birds may now have all outgrown the nest. Or do you want financial success or to down-size your life to have more time for yourself, friends or family? Do you want or need financial security or are you one of life's gypsies and it is those around you for whom possessions are important? Take time to identify and answer your questions.

The negative aspect arises if you feel you are working to maintain an edifice or situation that has lost its meaning – so step off the wheel and assess if these are valid feelings or exhaustion speaking.

The Seven of Cups

So many choices, so many thoughts of what might have been and still could be. The Seven of Cups examines questions of emotional satisfaction, what would make you happy, and generally cards of choice appear either when you are feeling restless or when your life needs a different emphasis.

With Cups, relationships are often the focus and sometimes love and happiness can become more important than success or independence. Remember, however, that they are not mutually exclusive. But the card also talks of less tangible emotional fulfilment through spiritual evolution, whether healing powers that are strongly linked with Cups through the development of divinatory abilities, or heightened predictive powers. You have so many potential paths and if you allow your heart to guide you and follow your heart, you will make the right choices.

The only danger lies in allowing Fate to make the decisions or in the illusion that we can have it all.

The Seven of Wands

The Seven of Wands comes down to principles and ideals and how far you can compromise to keep the peace or fit in with others whom you may like, but who have very different values and lifestyles.

Some see this as a lonely card or one involving fighting off opposition – I myself have emphasised this aspect in the past. But it is primarily a card of independence, of being sufficiently confident to stand by what you believe in, to follow your own star, even if it is not the one others focus on. Your original vision, altruism and drive promise that in any aspect of life your presence will have a positive effect, whether you are spearheading a campaign against pollution, writing a play or book with a social or spiritual message, capturing abstract concepts on canvas or in clay, or communicating your ideas in a thousand different ways. Right now you may feel as if you have an audience of one, but most great people started by convincing themselves first, so believe in yourself as you take the plunge and watch the ripples spread outwards.

The negative aspect comes in trying to fight the unenlightened on their own less noble terms – you are worth so much more.

The Seven of Swords

When the moon is almost gone and there is darkness, nasty things can creep out of the woodwork, things that would not dare confront you directly by light of day.

There may be deceit or spite around you, jealousy and backbiting amongst neighbours, colleagues, employees, people you meet socially – even sometimes in healing or psychic circles where jealousies can run high. People may feel threatened by your spirituality and your refusal to join in power or ego games or their

petty world with its emphasis on what you have and how you look. If you are working on your spiritual development, you may encounter also scepticism, logic taken beyond the bounds of open-minded reason, even among family or friends who do not understand the changes in you.

So you may feel isolated, but there are like-minded people who can support you. In the meantime, visualise your swords as gleaming blades extending outwards to keep you safe from barbs and jibes or small-mindedness.

The Eights

✛

The Eights are ruled by Saturn and can mirror frustrations and limitations that may lead to abandoning not only what may be redundant, but situations that could be salvaged. However, more positively, they may refer to movement and adapting to new skills and situations. Saturn himself was deposed by his sons, after trying to hold back the natural progression of events. He was sent to Italy, where he taught the farmers agriculture and engineering, and established a Golden Age of peace and plenty.

The Eight of Pentacles

This is often called the 'apprentice card' and can indicate a change in career, especially where new skills will be required. But it also talks of any new form of learning, whether this may be artistic, spiritual, literary or technological, or up-grading computer skills, DIY, taking a driving test or applying for a pilot's licence. For the energies of Saturn are driving you to widen your scope and maybe also gain new sources of income as well as expertise.

Adaptability is the key to the Eight of Pentacles and, whatever the challenge in your domestic or financial life, your natural curiosity to find better and more fulfilling ways of organising your world augur a busy but fruitful period, one in which home improvements or car maintenance are more likely than uprooting yourself or buying new transport. It is a time for doing, not dreaming, and you may surprise yourself at how adept you are at fixing everything from chaotic finances to a recalcitrant state-of-the-art computer.

The only negative aspect of this card is not applying your new-found knowledge to make tangible improvements in your life.

The Eight of Cups

Saturn and Cups do not make a happy marriage and this signifies a dark night of the soul, showing a waning moon and usually a hooded figure heading off into the night.

Perhaps you have reached an emotional impasse when the old arguments have gone round in so many circles you are dizzy and you want to clear the decks. Sometimes the solution is to abandon a relationship that is no longer giving joy and to move on; but this card usually refers to a past, not current, unresolved situation that you still carry in your heart.

What is more, most Eight of Cups cards depict the departing figure leaving behind not friends, lover or children, but Cups filled to overflowing with old redundant emotions. It may be time for an emotional spring-clean and for burying those bones that have no more life or even resentment left in them. If you are feeling jaded, it may be time for you to take a holiday, change your place of residence or free yourself from restricting emotional ties. You do not have to abandon your ageing parents or hypochondriac friend, just put more emotional – and maybe physical – distance between you.

The problem is one you have met before in the Tarot: if you move away from disappointment or dissatisfaction with those around you, instead of trying to tackle the problem, you will simply find that you have carried the problems with you, because you have failed to make the necessary changes within.

The Eight of Wands

This is sometimes called the 'up-and-flying' card because in many packs the wands are flying through the air. It is certainly the fastest-moving image in the Tarot pack and if you are planning to move house or change your job or have booked a trip far or near, these energies will have you positively sprinting to the travel or estate agent, throwing open the windows of your home and your life, and maybe making on-the-spot decisions about many aspects of your world which are in need of renovation.

Since Saturn is involved, you can be fairly certain that some obstacle or setback was or is in some way implicated in all this movement – but like Saturn this really will be your Golden Age, whether you are 16 or 60, if you seize every opportunity as it presents itself.

Now is the time to book a course on scuba-diving or exploring past lives, perhaps both, and to cast off the old prohibitions, inhibitions and self-restrictions. These changes you make now will have long-term positive implications, and situations or people who have held you back will be less intrusive or at least less vociferous and your confidence levels will soar.

The only negative aspect arises if you do not resolve problems and clear the decks before you introduce innovation.

The Eight of Swords

This is definitely the child of Saturn and, like earlier Swords cards, speaks of fears and restrictions. This is an extension of the negative aspect of the previous card. You may have taken an initial step towards improvement, but the past still seems to hold you back.

It is very easy to believe that all the restrictions are in your head, and with positive thinking you can release yourself from the thrall of the past. I myself accepted that interpretation of this card until very recently. But that is an illusion, that we can and should do whatever we want and walk away from anything or anyone who holds us back. However, life is rarely that simple. The loving, caring nature of most women makes it very hard for them to say: 'That is not my responsibility and it's not my fault.'

But the Eights are cards of movement and if you can pluck up courage to go into the wild wood of whatever it is you most fear that is holding you prisoner, it probably will not have half as many perils as those you have conjured up in the long nights. In that way you can free yourself.

The Nines

✛

The Nines are ruled by Mars and since nine is the last single digit, it is a very magical number, signifying perfection. The nines are brimming with courage, determination to succeed whatever the odds, self-reliance and independence – the cards of the evolved self. Their theme is that of the separate person, not in the sense of the High Priestess who is separate from the world, but one who has strong self-identity within the world. Though she may have good and permanent relationships, she does not need others to define her place or purpose. Some women achieve this state at its most positive while quite young, but for others, myself included, it may take many years of trying to be what others want us to be, before accepting and valuing what we are.

The Nine of Pentacles

The Nine of Pentacles usually features a richly dressed woman in a garden filled with pentacles that represent the harvest of what she has sown. But she is not just a woman who earns her own money, nor does she necessarily live alone. The card talks of being complete in ourselves and not being persuaded by popular images or the consumer society into conforming to a particular image or lifestyle.

Some young women have this independent focus from early on – both my daughters possess this ability to live on their own terms, whereas I struggled from one trend to another, somehow just missing them all. The card may appear if your financial or domestic arrangements are under scrutiny or you are being criticised by those who resent or are worried by the fact that you are not bound by the need to conform to their standards. The garden of pentacles is still growing, not set out neatly as trophies in the living room.

Of course it is an excellent card to select if you are undertaking a financial venture or moving into your own home, as it promises material success and security. But it may also appear when financial or material independence may be an issue. You may be considering going into partnership, moving in with or sharing domestic and financial resources with a lover or close friend. You may be worried that commitment might take away your independence or that a future house-mate or partner in love or business may be financially unreliable. If there are fears, it is important to examine them, as they may be valid.

The negative aspect appears when your workload has left you isolated and you feel that there is no spontaneity or simple pleasure in your life.

The Nine of Cups

The Nine of Cups is another card of self-confidence, but the self-reliance here is directed towards emotional detachment. That may be no bad thing, for if we love and value ourselves, then we can enter into loving relationships without needing to use other people to act as anchors in storms, or as resident psychotherapists or to keep boosting our ego 24 hours a day.

If we are happy in our own company, possessiveness is not an issue and we are not afraid to let friends and family go, knowing that they will return willingly. It is the card that at its best reflects the ability to be centred spiritually and to have inner as well as outer harmony.

You may be at a time in your life when you are still searching for the right person, but nevertheless have a rich emotional life. Relationships, although happy, may temporarily need less input than the fulfilment of a particular dream or ambition or demands of career. You may not want to settle for second-best emotionally or have fears or doubts about a commitment, in which case you should take your feelings very seriously, as generally fears without basis reside in the Sword cards.

The only danger comes in emotional isolation that may result from demanding perfection in others and seeking ideal love rather than a real person.

The Nine of Wands

Here it is the courage of Mars in adversity that is the focus, since the image usually centres around a guy standing alone, 'bloody but unbowed'. The separateness here is not necessarily from choice, but may represent a hard struggle, whether personal, spiritual or in your career, in which you have had to fight in the past or are still fighting to gain success against considerable odds.

But this card may question the purpose of all your endeavours, whether you will ever be or have what lies at the end of your personal rainbow. The answer is that success is assured if you keep your courage and determination and carry on. But you do need rest, for the Nine of Wands is closely linked with your health and stress-related illnesses can be a way of telling you to slow down. The apparent negativity in a card may reflect not specific events, but the stage you have reached when even the fiery Wands can run out of steam.

The Nine of Swords

The Nine of Swords is the card of the insomniac who fights so many battles in her head during the night that when the morning comes she has used all her finest arguments and has no strength for the actual (or imagined) fight.

This is a card that says you may be feeling isolated – yet another of the 'fears in your head' variations on the theme of self-doubt, the ongoing theme that runs through the swords. Yet pick any Nine of Swords in a pack with an illustrated Minor Arcana and you will see the swords themselves do not point towards the woman who sits up in bed hiding her eyes after yet another nightmare.

Swords represent Air, the direction of the dawn and the season of Spring in magic, so let the light of day and the ascending energies drive away all the spectres. Above all, in this isolation card, find someone sympathetic to communicate with – and learn to believe in yourself.

The Tens

✛

Tens herald completion. I used to identify them with Pluto and his ability to transform what is redundant into a new, more perfected form and that association is still valid. However, it is the first of the joint numbers, made out of the original nine. The figure 10 is formed from the 0 (the Fool in many packs) of unmanifest power, which has now evolved through the nine numbers. The 1 in the figure 10 marks the next and higher stage. Tens are associated with Isis and Osiris, the I and O. Osiris was ritually killed and dismembered by his brother Seth and his body re-formed and brought back from the dead by Isis, his sister-wife, the Mother Goddess. This rebirth was essential as the core of the annual Corn God sacrifice–rebirth ritual carried out to ensure that the Nile would flood each year and fertilise the soil.

These images capture the deeper significance of the Ten cards, which can represent either a state of unified perfection and fulfilment (as opposed to the solitary perfected self of the Nines) or endings before new beginnings and the transformative state that links the two.

They are connected also with the Chinese belief that nothing is static and that extreme joy and extreme sorrow are polarities and when the one state is attained, it overflows into the other. So when you reach ten, or draw your Ten card in a reading, you do not collect the jackpot and go home to a life of luxury and endless pleasure. Life rarely stands still and often, as soon as we have arrived, we find ourselves en route to a new destination. Indeed, those who suddenly attain wealth may experience great unhappiness when, having bought everything and seen everything, they find the challenge of life has gone (however, if any reader has a spare million, I would be happy to be proved wrong).

The Ten of Pentacles

The Ten of Pentacles portrays domestic bliss and material security. But since the cards are symbolic, this card refers to whatever would make you happy, the home you would like and the kind of life you would enjoy.

In spite of the traditional and quite patriarchal imagery of this card, the meaning lies in reassuring you that you are on course and that whether you live alone or with 20 assorted relatives or student friends, in an Antarctic base camp, 5,000 miles from the nearest settlement or in a crowded suburban road in south-east London, it is a necessary part of your life. For home in this sense is the place where you can be yourself. If life seems mundane, then it is time to give your present world a face-lift, rather than moving on to a new one.

The card can also indicate imminent financial success. This may not refer to an inheritance or lottery win, but some work or enterprise you have undertaken that may bring financial gain beyond your reasonable expectations.

The negative aspect arises only if the bricks and mortar become more important than the people, or the journey more important than the arrival.

The Ten of Cups

The Ten of Cups gives the same message on the emotional plane. The way to happiness lies through stable relationships, togetherness and family bliss rather than romantic love and extra-curricular passion. I used to dislike this card intensely, seeing it as some idealised 'advertisement' family. But now I realise that it is really talking about the desire to have a committed relationship, not necessarily involving children, and I observed that the card frequently appeared in the readings of feisty young women who had their life and work planned to the last detail. Six months later, they would phone me to report that they had met Mr or Ms Right.

Equally, women in their sixties or seventies who were widowed, divorced or confirmed spinsters would select the card and laugh at suggestions of a possible attachment, but they too must have been giving out love vibrations, because the card worked its magic in almost every case. The card may appear when you are alone but feel it's time to settle down. If you are already in a stable relationship, this promises even greater joy. But it may also represent the need to make a deeper commitment in a developing relationship or to give a partner, child or parent more time.

The only drawback inherent in the Tens is when you prefer to wait for the Knight in shining armour to appear, rather than seeing potential (if less exciting) lovers in those whom you meet at work or at the delicatessen counter on Saturday mornings.

The Ten of Wands

The Ten of Wands talks of a heavy burden or worry that is soon to be lifted. The good thing about this card is that the best is yet to come and you are in that transition–transformation period, also reflected in the next card, when you can see the light at the end of the tunnel.

You may have worked very hard for recognition, promotion or less tangible forms of reward or to benefit others but found that recognition always seems to be coming next week or next month – or even further away. You should accept and acknowledge your own personal achievements when you select this card, even if others do not. Remember, regardless of the old saying, tomorrow does come and with it the happiness or success you deserve.

The negative aspect is when you do not enjoy the lesser successes you achieve on the way – and fail to shed unnecessary burdens, not least your own high expectations of yourself and what constitutes fulfilment.

The Ten of Swords

The Ten of Swords is sometimes called the darkest hour before the dawn and here the swords do pierce the victim. But dawn is breaking and to regard the card as gloomy is to mistake its deeper significance.

I mentioned earlier the myth of Isis and Osiris and many cultures have a Corn God who willingly sacrifices himself so that the land will be fertile. Shamans, the magic men and women in many cultures, undergo a ritual death and are re-formed in a more perfect, permanent state by the ancient Bone Goddess, taker but also giver of life. So on a personal level you may select this card when you are desperately fighting a lost cause or hanging on to a dead relationship or stage in your life. It is time to accept that some aspect of your life is ending and allow yourself to be sad and rest before moving on.

It also talks of a spiritual transformation, through your unfolding psychic world, so that you do see the world in a different way. It is a card of transformation, of fertility, new life, hope and a richer understanding of the interconnectedness of people and the natural spheres, enlightenment that will increase as you evolve.

DAY 22
The Court Cards – the Pages

⁜

The Court Cards on first examination appear in almost every pack to be quite static and stylised and in a sense they are, for they are templates of people who are significant in our lives. The suits signify the areas to which they apply. But as you read the descriptions, you will find that you can identify not only for example your partner, your mother, your best friend, your younger brother and even the office dragon, but also aspects of yourself in the different roles you occupy at various times during the day and your life. As you use the Court Cards, you become aware of how, by adopting a different persona in specific situations, you can boost your authority or allow gentler parts of your nature to shine through.

There are 16 Court Cards, four for each suit, that may have different titles and, in the case of the Pages and Knights, different roles. They form the bridge between the archetypal cards of the Major Arcana and the more specific Minor Arcana cards, revealing the personalities and personal reactions to actual situations.

Traditionally, the Court Cards are applied to real-life characters, according to external characteristics, so that the King of Pentacles might be a staid but reliable and kindly guy of middle years or beyond. Recognise your bank manager, your father or even your partner? But it is not that simple. We all know a charismatic 50-year-old Knight of Cups married to patient, capable Queen of Pentacles: his ageing boyish charm catapults him from one chivalrous flirtation to another while she worries about the mortgage and unblocks the drains.

Where the Knights and Pages are concerned, there may be even more confusion. If you have younger children, you may identify them with the Page cards and the Knights with children who are grown up. But if you are female and under 35 with a partner the same age, you might see yourself in matters of love and Tarot love-spells as a Page and your guy as a Knight, unless he is an older man. In a single-sex relationship, one partner might occupy the animus role and the other the anima or you may view yourselves as different suits of Knights or Pages.

And, as I said, you carry within you aspects of all the Court Cards. You are the King of Wands when you are upgrading the computer equipment at work or seeking orders from new territories. If you are 60 and have fallen in love, but feel very unsure, you may be a Page of Cups, although if you are making the running with a guy who is slow on the romantic uptake, you may have to assume the Knight's role. Think of the cards as a series of masks or costumes that you and the people in your world adopt at various times to express certain innate qualities.

Complex? Only if you stick to conventional categories. Used intuitively, the Court Cards can offer many clues as to the dynamics of any group, from the workplace to the health club.

The Pages

Although I have referred to the Page as 'he' throughout this chapter, the Page conventionally refers to a child or younger teenager of either sex or an adult female under 35. When you are reading a spread, the association will usually come rapidly to mind, unless it is a person who is about to come into your life. But if the link is not clear, reinterpret the Page as an aspect of your own personality or that of the questioner, perhaps as an yet undeveloped aspect or strength. The Page can also emerge when you are beginning or hoping to begin a new relationship, career move or even a new direction.

On a more negative note, Pages can represent a person of any age who is childish.

The Page of Pentacles

This Page is everyone's favourite child or grandchild: loyal, reliable, intensely practical, kind and considerate and a tower of strength in troubled times. It can also refer to a loyal friend or colleague whom you do not mind seeing on a 'bad hair' day and who will take you for some retail therapy and add brandy to the tea that goes with the sympathy.

The card may appear when you feel in need of someone who makes you feel good about yourself. Or you may be planning a simpler, perhaps slower, way of life, maybe beginning a new practical or financial venture or new domestic arrangement and you feel uncertain.

The card is only negative if your particular Page of Pentacles, who may be of any age, constantly finds himself (or it may be herself) in one avoidable practical or financial mess after another and relies on others – usually you – to sort out the latest crisis.

The Page of Cups

The Page of Cups is the dreamer: kind, sympathetic, easily hurt and sensitive to the needs of others. Maybe this is a child or a female under 35 who weeps over the sorrows of strangers, especially if they are four-footed, and who may suffer from stress-related illnesses because of this acute sensitivity to the world.

Your Page of Cups will remember the unofficial anniversaries, the day a loved one died or your divorce came through, and will just listen – and cry or laugh with you. Expect sentiment rather than high romance and passion – many a lasting relationship has started with a guy who is a Page of Cups at heart, whatever his age, who will walk miles through the rain to help you start the car – although usually you end up fixing it yourself – and will give you fluffy toys or real kittens instead of raunchy underwear.

The only negative aspect is in the tendency to idealise others and be blind to faults – if the current hero or heroine offers criticism or is off-hand, the Page may suffer physically as well as mentally; so if you are the Page, do not wear your heart on your sleeve.

The Page of Wands

PAGE of WANDS.

The Page of Wands is the original free spirit – quick-witted, curious, imaginative and eager to try anything new. His ideals are untainted by the desire for success and enthusiasm for life is unbounded. Whether a young person or a female friend or the naïve but lovely guy in your life who loves new gadgets but cannot understand a bus timetable, this Page brings joy, fun and laughter and will always have a surprise or an outing secretly planned.

This Page often has personal associations; he brings that inner bubble of joy that reconnects us with simple pleasures, with the curiosity to explore new fields and new ideas and above all those half-formed plans that, as yet, live only in our imaginations, but may have great implications in the future. Imagination is the greatest gift of the Page of Wands and may open the door to psychic and spiritual exploration.

The downside is that this Page, whatever his age, is easily discouraged and if the pieces of life's jigsaw do not instantly fit, he will throw away the puzzle and try something new.

The Page of Swords

This is the old head on young shoulders who worries endlessly about everything from the environment to the interest rate on his savings. Not an easy child or friend, but one who demonstrates fierce loyalty and would defend to the death you or any cause he considered just.

PAGE of SWORDS.

The Page of Swords is clever, observant and humorous and any misdirected aggression is motivated by fear or righteous anger attached to the wrong cause. Uncertainty can make him seem devious and careless of other's feelings, so you really will need to handle this Page with tact and kindness. Your embryo teenager, even if he is approaching 60, is bursting with unanswered questions that require the wisdom of Solomon to resolve. But this Page will, if directed positively, use the gifts of a logical mind and focus to overcome inertia and injustice.

This is a card that can also reflect your own sense of helplessness about unfair treatment or a disappointment – it is important to defend yourself from the barbs of small-minded people.

The negative side occurs when the Page unintentionally hurts others by attacking the wrong people out of a sense of frustration and through inner pain.

DAY 23

The Knights

✢

The Knights of the Tarot are true knights in shining armour, dashing after one Grail or another and not pausing for breath but full of movement, enthusiasm and drive in both relationships and ventures. Traditionally, Knights are either older teenagers or men under 35. A Knight can also be a partner or friend of either sex who is adult but still free from responsibility.

A Knight can represent a facet of your personality, a project or relationship that is quite new, but to which you feel totally committed. Therein lies the negative aspect of the Knights, who pursue their own desires at the expense of others.

The Knight of Pentacles

The Knight of Pentacles is the most stable and static of the knights, tempering restlessness and crusading with a strong vein of reality and a respect for the world as it is. He may be a natural environmentalist and, unusually for the Knights, tends not to ride his horse through the fields at full speed, because of the possible danger of damage to the crops and wildlife.

So, whether the Knight is an older teenager, a man you know who is under 35 or indeed any man or woman who is uncommitted to a stable relationship, this card augurs positive interactions and creative input that

KNIGHT of PENTACLES

can kindle your own enthusiasm, especially for an area of life you had considered unproductive or dull. He will produce results and not just fine speeches or vague promises. As a lover, he will be loyal and understanding, but maybe he will need stirring to passion.

In your own life, this Knight promises that the cause or project about which you are waxing lyrical does have firm foundations and will succeed if you structure your enthusiasm into a realistic time frame.

The only negative aspect is if this Knight forgets he or she is a Knight and fails to explore potential avenues, so imposing unnecessary limitations on future possibilities.

The Knight of Cups

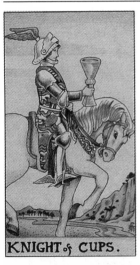

KNIGHT of CUPS.

The Knight of Cups is the quintessental, chivalrous knight, who seeks perfection in self and others and especially in love. This is the poet, the musician, the Seeker after Truth, and for him there may be many Holy Grails to follow, many fair maidens and many golden tomorrows. This can be a mindset that guys in particular can get stuck in, which can make them wonderful lovers, but not necessarily reliable or enduring partners.

As this Knight, you focus on what is of meaning in your life, and this will not necessarily be love. The card talks of the urge to follow your heart and to fulfil your dreams, which may not be about mundane things like mortgages and tiling the bathroom, but about far-off places, whether actual or imagined, and people to whom you can relate spiritually, as well as emotionally.

The only negative aspect of this Knight is inconstancy in affections, partly caused by finding that the beloved is only human.

The Knight of Wands

This is the archetypal knight of legend, who follows the perilous path without regard for personal hardship or danger. The Knight of Wands is the great communicator, creator and inspiration to others, the innovator who devises brilliant schemes and loves travel and risk of any kind.

Should this Knight enter your life, whether as an older teenager, an enthusiastic work colleague or the guy or gal of your dreams, you will need to have your mobile phone, fax and e-mail ready and be prepared to travel, talk and work all night, if necessary, to cram in every moment of the technicolour world into which you have been propelled.

This is an especially empowering card to have for personal motivation. Whatever ideas you have, whatever original slants on old questions, whatever vague plans to travel or expand your business empire, now is the time to initiate them; with your communicative and persuasive powers gleaming like the sun, you will inspire others with enthusiasm. Enjoy present happiness and if it is not in evidence create joy from within.

The negative aspect is a tendency to be economical with facts – not lying exactly, but putting an imaginative slant on reality.

The Knight of Swords

This knight is not as dark as he is conventionally painted. A younger and less spiritually-focused version of the Magician, he is a terrific catalyst for change, challenging the status quo and confronting inertia or the woolly-brained thinking of others.

There is no lack of courage whether in yourself or in others. The Knight of Swords will demolish the restricting Tower and unmask the Devil lurking in the shadows and is an excellent antidote to

KNIGHT of SWORDS .

oversentimentality or unbridled emotion. If you have been under great provocation or strain from others, this card will endow you with the power to turn challenge into advantage. This knight has great organisational qualities, planning any action like a military operation, but may also in the process steamroller others into agreement or simply push aside those with a different world view.

And this leads to the negative aspect, a tendency to disregard the feelings of others and even to be malicious if crossed.

DAY 24
The Queens

✥

The Queens usually are interpreted as more mature women, whether mothers or female authority figures, symbolising female fertility and wisdom. They may appear alongside the Empress in readings, showing in what area of your life your nurturing tendencies are manifest.

Some women become Queens in the maturity stakes before they leave school, while others may be struggling to attain or are still resisting the Wise Woman phase when girl-power has been replaced by mobility aid.

Guys too who acknowledge their caring gentle, receptive side have these qualities. The key to understanding the Queens lies in discovering what keeps each one on their particular throne – necessity or choice.

The negative aspect is in possessiveness or living other people's lives for them.

The Queen of Pentacles

As a chaotic soul, I have in the past been less than appreciative of the positive and empowering side of this Queen, regarding her as queen of hearth and home and disregarding her first-rate practical and organisational skills, not to mention her ability to plan her finances and to make others welcome wherever she is.

She cares for the sick, the old and the troubled, not by dispensing advice but with practical input, the creative giver whose home we all love to visit, especially if we are feeling in need of tender, loving care, the hub of many people's world both professionally

QUEEN of PENTACLES

and socially. But she is so much more and routinely makes things happen on many levels. She may be a top executive who understands that good working conditions and an awareness of the needs of individuals make for a smooth-running workplace. She keeps to deadlines, demanding only of others what she does herself.

At home this Queen is the same, so that whether she lives on a boat or in an apartment overlooking Central Park or entertains you at her workplace or a special venue, she will always take the time and care to make you feel that you matter to her. On a personal level, this quality may be seen in your life as the ability to draw together many disparate strands in a way that appears effortless, though you know differently. You may find that your time is very much in demand, so you must be careful not to overstrain yourself.

And this can be the weak link. If the Queen takes on too many responsibilities, she can become exhausted and enter martyr mode. She must then decide if she is really expressing her own need to be cared for when she rushes around in fulfilling others' every need.

The Queen of Cups

This is the archetypal Queen who gives love, support and approval to all through every aspect of her being and if upset she will feel, and sometimes become, ill in mind, body and soul, like the vulnerable Page of Cups.

Whether you are the Queen or she is someone close to you, the Queen of Cups is the agony aunt of the universe, the person to whom strangers on trains and planes tell their innermost secrets. She is a natural clairvoyant, dowser and superb Tarot reader, who reads people as easily as the cards and answers unspoken questions. She regularly detects friends' and family's distress psychically and can be especially sensitive to negative atmospheres, to the detriment of her own health. Her love of harmony makes her an oasis of calm for the troubles of others and, if this is you, you must take care that you give as much love to yourself as you accept from others. As a personal characteristic, she may also represent fertility in the widest sense.

How can such a lovely lady have any negative attributes? Only if she derives her emotional satisfaction from mending and nurturing other people's relationships, rather than her own.

The Queen of Wands

The Queen of Wands is the archetypal Wise Woman, Grandmother Spider in the Native North American tradition, who makes the interconnections between life and people and also makes sure the network is not only up and running but also in supersonic mode. She may produce a novel a month, while organising the local branch of Greenpeace and making her home a hive of activity and creativity.

She does not live through or solely for her family, though she may be happily married and a mother. She is probably a natural healer and, like the Queen of Cups, an excellent Tarot reader, though she taps into cosmic and natural energies and so is also a gifted spell-caster.

If this Queen's energies are to the fore of your personal qualities right now, you are moving into a particularly creative period in which elements that were previously conflicting will come together and you will be able to see the pattern of your life, perhaps for the first time, linked with others, but also rooted in your personal power base and focus.

The challenging aspect of this Queen is not to lose patience with those who lack vision or who are resistant to change, perhaps through fear.

The Queen of Swords

QUEEN of SWORDS.

You may have several candidates to fill this role: your mother-in-law or your own mother, a critical neighbour, your partner's ex-wife or girlfriend, a jealous colleague or discouraging teacher. Dig deeper and you may find a betrayed or disappointed woman, whose own sorrows make her bitter and over-critical. She may prove to be one of life's natural wicked witches, but if you give her the benefit of the doubt, at least you have untangled your own negativities and projections from her clouded aura.

If you identify any part of yourself with this card, see if you can unload some of those factors that have given you a temporarily jaundiced eye on the world. You may be entirely justified in your current world view but, since positivity breeds positivity and vice versa, if you can let go of some of the sorrows that ensnare you, you can begin to re-establish new and happier interconnections, that allow your true self to shine through.

Even the negative side of the Queen of Swords is not malicious. Perhaps out of desperation or sheer unhappiness, she may be tempted to resort to emotional blackmail when she should be letting go of a no-win relationship.

The Kings

⁜

The Kings traditionally represent mature or older men or male authority figures, embodying power, achievement, justice, wisdom and responsibility – and, of course, the inevitable frustrating paternalistic qualities that have women wanting to scream.

Some people do automatically associate a King with their father, boss or husband, just as they automatically see the Queen as a mother figure. But of course the Kings are also empowering cards for women, representing our animus side, our power and drive to succeed, linked with ambition and wisdom, but of the solar, traditional and left-brained kind, rather than lunar insights of the 'Wise Woman' type of Queen.

Kings can actually be male or female, young or old, although maturity and power are built into their character.

The Kings' challenging aspects are their domineering ways and inflexibility.

The King of Pentacles

The King of Pentacles is the card of success in the world's terms: recognition, status and a platinum credit card or three, whose balance is paid off early every month. If he is a guy you know, he will be firmly rooted in his domestic world, of which he sees himself as benign lord and master. At work, he will have photographs of his family and dogs in silver frames on his desk. Conventional to the core, hard-working and generous, what he lacks in excitement he compensates for in wisdom and compassion, and he can fix everything from your eccentric

KING of PENTACLES

plumbing to your portfolio of shares – or your overdraft. He is the friendly bank manager, the honest estate agent or wise older person who tempers experience with compassion. You can rely on this guy when he turns up in your life or your reading – and remember, this King is not necessarily a man!

If you identify this King with yourself, the way to the success, security or recognition you desire is through the conventional route, sheer hard work and perseverance all the way to the platinum cards. If you are financially footloose and fancy-free, the card may advise caution and accumulation rather than speculation.

This King's only drawback is in his resistance to innovation; he may want to go on vacation to the same resort he has been every summer since he was a solemn little boy clutching his piggy bank. But at least his stolid constancy means he will never let you down.

The King of Cups

KING of CUPS.

Very different is the King of Cups for whom you will wait on many train stations while he listens to someone else's tale of woe or watches the sunset on a completely different station and vaguely wonders where you are.

But you will forgive him, for he is the most charismatic of the Kings and will turn up two hours late with a bouquet of roses. Popular and benign, he puts people above property or achievement and his inner world is as important as the outer one. He may be spiritual, religious or involved in the caring professions, but invariably he is the dreamer who believes in the goodness of humanity and is constantly striving for perfection. At its best, this is a card where family and partners can feel secure because the King is happiest when he is supporting and protecting those he loves.

In a reading, you may identify this King in yourself if you are seeking a deep emotional commitment or if you have dreams that are so powerful that you know you must fulfil them or you will wither away emotionally. The message is to follow your heart, and to find happiness – this may be with another person or it may be in pursuit of your spiritual destiny.

The only negative aspect here resides in a tendency towards depression and an inability to stand against injustice – this King hates to upset anyone. He is also inclined to idealise unattainable women, which can be infuriating for his current partner.

The King of Wands

The King of Wands could sell refrigerators at the North Pole, because he has perfected those entrepreneurial qualities seen in the Knight of Wands. He or she – for a remarkable number of these Kings are female – is not to be found tending the garden, though he could design a water feature to rival Niagara, if he could remain in the same place long enough.

Creative, technologically orientated, energetic, optimistic and eager to share his considerable knowledge and wisdom, he is a man of vision and ideals and the driving force behind many ventures. He lives life to the full and expects others to do the same; he loves travel and may move house frequently. This is the card of career and ambition to succeed in any field on the very fast track – preferably by unusual or unconventional means.

This can be a woman's personal card if she has had many false starts and about-turns. Sometimes these powerful, creative tendencies are hard to harness and direct. But once focused, they promise that whether you are considering a career-change or boost, a step towards independent action or a sudden brilliant scheme that inspires you to work harder than ever before and still enjoy every minute. You have the drive and initiative to make a real impression on the world – and maybe in some area turn conventional thinking on its head.

The only negative facet appears if the King becomes totally absorbed in some grandiose scheme and neglects everyday affairs.

The King of Swords

KING of SWORDS.

This King may be an unwelcome addition to a spread, associated with authority figures such as government officials, judges, lawyers and doctors, in their less benevolent aspects, as well as stern fathers and critical partners who attempt to rule over the domestic scene paternalistically and autocratically.

In fact, Kings of Swords do possess a strong sense of responsibility and sense of justice, but their insistence on logic and the unvarnished truth can make them less than comfortable employers or companions – and this applies equally to women who have these characteristics. A King of Swords will walk to hell and back for those he loves and this is the key to those gentle emotions that may have been locked away in childhood or because of a betrayal in love during adolescence.

As a personal characteristic, this King can give you the sheer drive, logic and determination, the ultimate focused Sky power that will drive him on against all odds to succeed in a survival situation or to protect his loved ones.

His negative aspects are pedantry and insensitivity to the feelings of others, which at worst may tip over into bullying behaviour.

DAY 26

Readings with Court Cards

✛

A Court Card reading with four cards

This is a spread that has grown out of a basic format I have used successfully for some years.

⊘ Shuffle only the 16 Court Cards and deal them out clockwise in a circle, face-down.

⊘ Select four cards, place them in a pile and shuffle them.

⊘ Dealing from the top, place one card close to you. Read this and then place a second card directly above the first, reading this before selecting the third, until you have the four cards in a vertical line.

| Card 4 | The person you will become |

| Card 3 | The person who will oppose you |

| Card 2 | The person who will help you |

| Card 1 | The person you are now |

These cards represent your present situation and the course on which you are set.

✪ Note these down and then collect the 16 Court Cards, shuffle them again, make the circle, select four more and arrange them as before.

This second layout will tell you what may happen if you allow someone else to change your course.

Card 1 – the person who you are now – will usually be different as this is the you seen through another's eyes.

✪ Note the cards in this layout.

✪ Take out the first Court Card that represented the person you are now (card 1) in the first layout and place that card as the first in a third layout.

✪ Shuffle the remaining 15 cards, again make the circle, deal as before but this time select only three cards for positions 2, 3 and 4.

This third layout will indicate what may happen if you follow your heart or instincts.

The interesting factor, since we all contain elements of all the Court Cards within us, is how the same card–role may appear in different positions in the three spreads according to who is dictating the course of your life. You can then assess whether you want to act or wait.

A 33-card spread for past, present and future

A friend used what was originally a 25-card spread for a life review for me and over the past nine years I have been quite astounded by the accuracy of the predictions, which came from the cards themselves and not from her knowledge of my life. During the past six months, however, I have discovered that by adding an extra eight cards on top of the eight cards of present factors, the next line of future possibilities can be made even more focused. Although you are using almost half the pack, it is the appearance and combination of cards in the specific rows that is significant, for the key to the spread as to our lives is the interconnection between past, present and future.

Use this spread only once for yourself and if you read for particular people regularly, do it only once for them, allowing time, not only to describe each card in detail, but to work on the interconnections and implications.

It is not a card formation to use with strangers, as unresolved issues both from the past and from present uncertainties can make this quite an emotive method.

Interpreting the 33-card spread

The first 24 cards

❂ Using the full pack, shuffle and deal the cards face-down as usual, with three rows of eight, from left to right.

❂ The nearest row to you will represent what has passed and is passing out of your life. The cards nearest the left-hand end of the row will refer to childhood and to more recent events towards the right of the row. This row may contain several unresolved issues, but more positively it also refers to those areas and people that have contributed to present success of happiness.

❂ The middle row is that of present influences and should also be read from left to right. In the present will reside relationships, home and work influences, personal current goals and achievements. This row tends to contain more conscious material, since the unconscious issues may be buried in the past line.

❂ The top row, furthest away from you, looks not at a set future, but potential ways forward. The immediate future will be to the left of the row and the distant future to the right.

You can, as I did, just use the first 24 cards and when you have read them, if you are not continuing with the next stage add one extra card, dealt face-down, that will identify the unexpected factor that will help your future success. Place this at the top of the reading, above the third row. You can get good readings using only the extra card at this first stage.

The eight strategy cards

These can be of use in identifying strategies to move from the present to the future in the most positive way and to avoid any potential hazards.

- Reshuffle what is left of the pack and deal eight cards, face-down, from left to right, on top of the middle line of cards so that each one covers one of the present cards.
- One by one, turn over the strategy cards and each will tell you how to get from the present to the future in connection with the issue contained in the card it covers.
- Then deal the last card at the top of the reading.

If this seems to be daunting or you feel overwhelmed by the sheer number of cards, simply start reading the cards as you would a story, changing tense with each row, from past to present to future and then, if you are using the extra cards, interpret each one as a strategy or solution.

DAY 27
A Calendar Spread

✛

This is an excellent spread to carry out for yourself and others, either at the beginning of the year, on an anniversary or birthday or at a significant change point in your life, as you can start the card wheel at any point.

○ Use the full pack of 78 cards.

○ Dealing from a shuffled pack, arrange the cards in a circle, in the following way: place the first two cards at the 12 o'clock position, face-down, and continue to arrange 11 more pairs of cards, one at each of the hour positions on an imaginary clock face.

○ Turn the cards over one pair at a time, beginning with the month at the top of the wheel. The first card for each month will give you helpful factors or positive trends and the second challenges to be overcome. You will usually find that each pair of cards naturally suggests an appropriate action or a time to let events take their course.

○ Read each pair before you turn over the next and you may see a month-by-month pattern emerging.

○ Finally, reshuffle what is left of the pack and select one card for the focus of the whole year.

○ Record the complete Calendar Spread in your Tarot diary and make notes each month how the spread links with the actual situation. It is usually very accurate.

Sheila's Calendar Spread

Sheila is in her late twenties and has been in the army since leaving school, since all her family had military connections. Next month she is leaving the service, much against her family wishes, as she is getting married to Ian, a civilian who runs a local craft shop near the army base and works as a part-time sculptor. They both want children as soon as possible and she does not want them to grow up as she did, moving from place to place. Sheila began her spread as the Old Year turned into the New.

January
Helpful aspects: The Ace of Wands
Challenges: The Four of Swords

Sheila is facing a new creative beginning in her married civilian life with this Ace and has already started to develop the interest in making pottery that originally drew her to Ian's shop. But she needs to recognise her own doubts expressed in the second card. Though she felt restricted in the army, there was security and she also fears her family's open disapproval of her new life-style. But the Four of Swords says these fears are worse in her mind than in reality.

February
Helpful aspects: The Four of Pentacles
Challenges: The Five of Pentacles

In February, Sheila will receive several thousand pounds as leaving payment from the army and Sheila and Ian have talked about putting a tiny pottery studio in the outbuildings where they can hold classes and demonstrations. But that would leave the couple with no savings. So the Four of Pentacles poses the question: should they hang on to the money or risk expansion?

The card of the Five of Pentacles shows beggars beneath a lighted church window being offered no help. An apparently gloomy challenge, but the card promises help from an unexpected source. Are there any local authorities or organisations who might help with a grant or loan?

March
Helpful aspects: The Six of Swords
Challenges: The King of Swords

The Six of Swords augurs moving into calmer waters and with an early Easter the tourist trade will have begun and with it easier financial times, so this is a card of the easing of worries.

Sheila identifies the King of Swords with her father, a fierce NCO who despises Ian because, in his opinion, he does not have a proper job, and blames him for taking Sheila away from the army.

But as Sheila and Ian become more settled together they will be able to face this obstacle to happiness.

April
Helpful aspects: The Ace of Swords
Challenges: The Six of Cups

The Ace of Swords represents a new beginning under difficulty and perhaps a new relationship with the King of Swords, as he comes to see his daughter is happy and making a success of her life. The Six of Cups may have Sheila looking back with rose-tinted spectacles at the past as the initial honeymoon period wears off, but this can be countered by looking at present and future happiness.

May
Helpful aspects: The Ace of Cups
Challenges: The Three of Pentacles

The Ace indicates that Sheila's thoughts may be turning to the children they both want as soon as possible and the challenge of the Three of Pentacles may refer to the actual structure of the new pottery, maybe a few teething troubles to be sorted out. A quiet month of consolidation and plans, with two steps forward and one back.

June
Helpful aspects: The High Priestess
Challenges: The Hermit

Sheila may discover in the Priestess her separate identity, not as an army daughter nor as Ian's wife but as what she herself wants. The danger expressed through the Hermit card is that Ian may see this as rejection and withdraw emotionally; but given increased communication of true feelings between the couple, Sheila may discover a separate area within the business in which she could develop her own talents, perhaps in developing the teaching aspect of the pottery.

July
Helpful aspects: The Empress
Challenges: The Two of Pentacles

The mothering–caring aspect comes to the fore with the Empress, maybe in connection with Sheila's desire to be a mother. The challenge is in trying to balance all the different demands of the shop, the pottery and making time for herself and Ian that is expressed in the juggler on the Two of Pentacles card. Is she ready to take on motherhood as well?

August
Helpful aspects: The Star
Challenges: The Devil

The busiest month for the shop and also one for Sheila and Ian to succeed in long-term ambitions, maybe to make plans for the future in the Star, a card of optimism for future fulfilment of their dreams.

The Devil is however diverting energy, keeping in all the negative and quite natural doubts, resentments and anxieties about Sheila's new way of life and anger at her parents for not being more supportive. Maybe it will be time for Sheila to speak out about her needs and fears to her parents.

September
Helpful aspects: The Sun
Challenges: The Moon

Happiness and success are assured this month with the Sun and the message to make every hour count, but there remains the question of the winter; it may be necessary to act, using the impetus of the Sun, not to take the easy lunar path of letting things take their course. However, the Moon is a creative card and so it may be that this ultimately holds the answer – maybe evening and day classes in the winter for locals, as Sheila suggested quite spontaneously when she saw the Moon card.

October
Helpful aspects: The Three of Cups
Challenges: The Six of Pentacles

The Three of Cups can represent a celebration or family occasion, a pregnancy, a coming-together of the family and reconciling differences. But the Six of Pentacles in a challenging aspect represents giving out more than is received, certainly financially and practically, so resources may be strained. Only if practical matters are resolved can emotional happiness be fully realised.

November
Helpful aspects: The Queen of Swords
Challenges: The Tower

The Queen of Swords is seen by Sheila as her mother who was forced to give up her own career in the army to have children, which she bitterly regretted. But in the helpful aspect she is perhaps mellowing and seeing that her daughter has not rejected her despite choosing her own way of life.

The Tower is a major softening of attitudes and an easing of financial problems, with an adjustment on all sides that may involve plain speaking and upheaval as Sheila moves from her family's shadow.

December
Helpful aspects: The Eight of Wands
Challenges: The Four of Wands

The Eight of Wands is an 'up and flying' card, of travel, moves and new challenges. Sheila says they have no plans to move for several years, but certainly there is movement around them, maybe in the new business opportunities.

The Four of Wands is a victory and happiness card, so any problems of the last couple of months will be resolved in time for Christmas but the ever-present challenge is in the question, 'What next?' And so it is a happy month, but one for looking to the future and not losing the initial impetus of the month.

Sheila became pregnant in July, the month of the Empress card. They did get a grant to expand, but in the following January the couple were offered a good price for the shop and pottery which they are considering as Ian has had some success as a sculptor. Sheila wants to take a pottery teaching course after the baby is born.

As for the final card, the trend of the year was the Ten of Cups, happiness in love and with family; after some major arguments, Sheila's parents have unexpectedly mellowed and her mother is helping in the shop. Her father has offered some financial input into the business which Ian and Sheila are considering. Both are excited about becoming grandparents.

Options and Pyramid Spreads

✛

An Options Spread reading

You can use this spread with a full pack, but it is one of the few spreads that does work when using the Minor Arcana alone or the Minor Arcana, plus Court Cards.

This is a very useful layout if you have two possible paths to follow and cannot decide which is best. Place your first card in the centre at the top, then add three cards below the left and three cards below the right of the top card to make two alternative pathways, or options.

The layout should look like this:

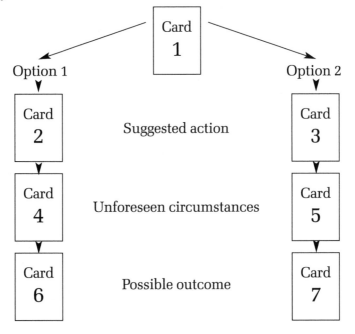

Card 1 identifies a question or area of concern you wish to consider. Cards 2 and 3 offer alternative actions or responses to the situation. Cards 4 and 5 suggest what unforeseen circumstances may be encountered in either case, and Cards 6 and 7 offer the two possible outcomes.

Maria's Options Spread

Maria is a Pisces, a dreamy, intuitive reflexologist and aromatherapist in her early forties who has recently joined a clinic run by a consortium of alternative practitioners. The advantage is that she is paid a regular salary, but Maria is worried by the commercialism and the increasing pressure to sell clients expensive products. Recently she was told that her sales figure was well below expectations and was asked to take on more clients. The result was that she felt she was not spending the extra time sometimes needed just talking to people who were experiencing difficulties in their lives. But if she leaves the practice, then she will have to start all over again and will face financial hardship.

Card 1 The Real Issue: The Ace of Pentacles

Card 2 Suggested Action for Option 1: The Devil

Card 3 Suggested Action for Option 2: The High Priestess

Card 4 Unforeseen Consequences of Option 1: Death

Card 5 Unforeseen Consequences of Option 2: The Two of Cups

Card 6 Possible Outcome of Option 1: The Three of Swords

Card 7 Possible Outcome of Option 2: The Three of Cups

The real issue, as represented by Card 1, all comes down to money. The Ace of Pentacles says that if Maria is to stay within the consortium, she needs to make money and that calls into question whether Maria can do this without compromising her principles, to give each individual as much care and time as they need.

Maria designated Option 1 as trying to adapt to a more commercial approach and Option 2 as not compromising her beliefs and accepting the consequences.

Suggested action (option 1)
The Devil indicates a fair amount of negativity and doubts about adopting a more money-orientated approach to healing. Maria is aware that she will need to suppress this if she is to maintain friendly relationships within the consortium and meet her new targets. But at what cost to her own spirituality – and ultimately her work?

Suggested action (option 2)
The High Priestess advises Maria to remain true to herself whatever the consequences, for it is her sensitivity and high ideals that have made her so successful in her work and brought her to the attention of her employers. This sensitivity makes her unable to conform to commercial pressures and so the card suggests working alone again, so that she can devote time to her patients.

Unforeseen circumstances (option 1)
Death augurs an ending. This may not only refer to the end of Maria's own path of gentle healing, but also perhaps to a diminishing of her natural abilities as she gives way to pressure and anxiety creeps in. Maria said this process had already started during the past few weeks.

Unforeseen circumstances (option 2)
The Two of Cups, a card of joining together with another person in an emotional or spiritual way. Maria understood this card instantly. On the day of the reading, Maria had been contacted by her friend Josie, a past-life therapist, who has a large house in the country that she runs as a healing sanctuary. Josie mentioned that she had a spare large studio and wondered if Maria would do some lecturing and demonstration sessions for her on a part-time basis. Might this be one way forward? Obviously Maria would

find it difficult to give up her full-time wage from the clinic, but she would be free to organise her own work.

Possible outcome (option 1)

The Three of Swords indicates the triumph of logic and, in this case, of commercial interests over emotion. This would suggest that Maria could succeed in her present post, if she could adopt a more detached attitude and see her work as a business enterprise. Because of her charismatic personality, she could easily sell products to her clients. But that would be success in terms of the consortium, which is at odds with her own commitment to her clients as people in need and not as a ready market for consumer interests.

Possible outcome (option 2)

The Three of Cups is another card of celebration and increase, and follows on directly from the previous Option 2 card. If Maria does go to work with her friend, whatever the initial financial hardships, she will find fulfilment and an increase in spiritual, if not actual, wealth. The card promises joy to others and to herself.

Maria did leave the consortium, and her new venture with Josie has, against all expectations, proved commercially viable and they are expanding the centre, but are keeping ther spiritual aims firmly to the fore.

The Pyramid Spread

Many clairvoyants use the Celtic Cross Spread as their *pièce de resistance* and I have myself taught it and described it in books several times. However, I much prefer the Pyramid Spread. It is no more ancient Egyptian than the Celtic Cross is Celtic and like the latter it takes its name from its shape. However, the pyramid is a sacred shape and in itself is said to contain great power.

The most famous pyramid that has been attributed special magical significance is the Great Pyramid of Cheops at Giza in Egypt, built around 2700 BC which seems to be the repository of inexplicable physical phenomena and also psychic and healing powers. It has been suggested that pyramids acted as transformers of cosmic energy.

Sleeping with a scale model pyramid beneath the bed, for example, not only increases energy levels the next day in many people, but also brings to a proportion of subjects lucid and predictive dreams and out-of-body sensations, especially ones connected with past lives. What is more, experiments demonstrate that sitting under a pyramid measurably increases the amplitude and frequency of alpha and theta brain waves that are naturally present in states of meditation and altered consciousness; this occurs even when subjects are blindfolded and unaware that an open pyramid structure has been lowered over them. Pyramids are also particularly female-friendly: in one study, women who slept under a pyramid for four to 16 weeks reported that they did not suffer menstrual cramps and pains and the actual time of menstruation was reduced.

The Pyramid Spread is one that works in practice with either the full pack or the Major Arcana and Number Cards, since you need a good range of cards to benefit from its insights.

Though it looks complicated, each step follows naturally and it consists of only ten cards.

Reading a Pyramid Spread

☻ Shuffle the pack and deal from the right, not the left as usual, in four rows, beginning from nearest to you or the questioner. The last row consists of a single card.

☻ Turn over each card and read it before turning over the next.

☻ If you find using specific positions hinders your natural reading ability, use the pyramid shape format and just read the cards as you would a story. This really does work well – sometimes on television, I will avoid using specific positions, as with a complex reading to complete in the assigned three minutes, I am aware that I could ruin the reading by concentrating on getting everything right, rather than on the needs of the viewer asking the question.

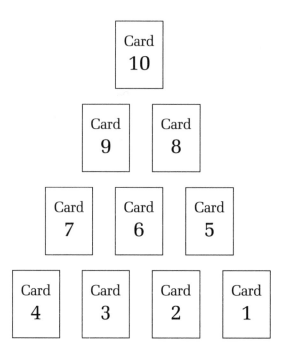

Card 1 The question: This may be posed either openly or consciously.

Card 2 The essence, sometimes called the Root of the Matter: This is the deeper, often unformed question or unconscious wish or fear.

Card 3 The head or logical considerations: In divination and magic, careful analysis that stems from deduction and detecting a pattern is a vital skill for the Tarot reader. Similarly, in any reading part of the equation involves what the conscious mind can deduce from given facts.

Card 4 The heart of the matter: This is what the questioner feels and while the emotional response alone is not the best indicator of possible action, what someone knows in their heart is right is too powerful an indicator to ignore.

Card 5 The price: Any decision, however positive, involves loss and regret for the options not taken and the cost, not only monetary but emotional, of any decision.

Card 6 Unhelpful influences: This can be any advice or criticism, however well-intentioned, any obstacles that stand in the way of fulfilling a goal or even self-doubts. Swords frequently turn up in this position.

Card 7 The unexpected: This is the card of seeing just over the next horizon to a factor that may affect your decision.

Card 8 Helpful influences: These may be friends, colleagues or an unexpected source or even your own special strengths that will enable you to succeed.

Card 9 Suggested action: A course that may alter or maintain the status quo, but which the questioner, rather than outside events, has decided.

Card 10 Possible outcome, the 'crown' of the reading: This card suggests possible consequences of the proposed action. It is not a card of fixed fate, because circumstances and our responses to them are constantly changing.

Rowan's Pyramid Reading

Rowan is a trained teacher in her mid-thirties and has three children. Her youngest son, Jim, has a learning disorder and has recently been offered a place at a new school that achieves excellent results, but this will mean her son being 50 miles from home for the school terms. Jim is only ten and has never been away from home; however, Rowan considers that the local schools are not suitable for Jim, as he is highly intelligent and is being badly bullied by other children.

Card 1 The conscious question: The Page of Cups
Is Jim old enough to face the emotional trauma of leaving home at such an early age? It is a real dilemma that needs to be weighed against his hopes of a successful future. The emotional consequences of staying and being bullied also weigh heavy.

Card 2 The unvoiced question: The Queen of Cups

Can Rowan bear to let Jim leave her? Rowan knows that the school is very homely and Jim has enjoyed his visits. But since Jim was small he has taken a great deal of her time and emotion and because he has no friends has remained much closer to her than a ten-year-old normally would be. She has given up her career, because the emotional aspects of Jim's disorder have meant that his schooling pattern has been irregular.

Card 3 The head of the matter: The World

For Jim, the school would be an expansion of his horizons and the chance to lead an independent life one day. Logically, Rowan knows that Jim needs to make friends and to move away from the loving but cloistered atmosphere of home.

Card 4 The heart of the matter: The Ace of Cups

Rowan says that she knows in her heart that it would be a new beginning for both of them, so that Jim could learn to form emotional attachments – and that she and Jim need to forge a new relationship, because he may feel his mother has betrayed him in sending him away – although he wants to go.

Card 5 The price: The Ace of Swords

The difficulties are highlighted in this card: Jim is going away at a relatively early age and Rowan feels unfounded guilt that she has somehow failed him. She is also aware that her marriage has deteriorated because of the constant struggle to get her younger son educated and she wonders what the future will hold.

Card 6 Unhelpful influences: The Queen of Swords

Rowan's mother-in-law blamed Rowan's bad management of Jim, although her other two children had no problems, saying that Harry, Jim's father, had also been clever but difficult, and that she had overcome the problems. This only added to Rowan's burden of guilt and sense of failure, because her mother-in-law even refused to accept the medical diagnosis confirming Jim's condition.

Card 7 The unexpected: The Ace of Wands

A third Ace in a reading would suggest the winds of change blowing strongly. Wands indicate a new beginning in career – could Rowan return to teaching in term-time while Jim was away? No, because that would be expected.

Card 8 Helpful influences: The King of Pentacles

Rowan identified this as her husband, who had been very supportive against his mother and in the various school crises. Could they now move closer in the extra time that would suddenly be released?

Card 9 Suggested action: The Eight of Pentacles

This is a card that appears a great deal in readings, because often the way out of difficulties is to learn a new skill or redirect an old one. Rowan had always wanted to convert her history degree into a doctorate so that she could work in a museum. But she went straight from college into teaching and then worked part-time until Jim's problems forced her to give up. Could this be the unexpected direction, since the local college had recently become affiliated to a university 100 miles away and now offered Masters degrees and doctorates under a distance-learning programme with residential weekends at the main university. This would have been impossible before Jim had been offered his place but now ...

Card 10 Possible outcome: The Sun

This indicated happiness through fulfilling potential for both Jim, if he went to the residential school, and for Rowan, if she took up her own life again.

Rowan agreed to let Jim go away for a term's trial and though they have both found it hard, the experiment seems to be working.

Magic and psychic awareness

✛

Although such techniques as meditation and visualisation have become enveloped in mystique and New Age jargon, they are routinely and totally unconsciously practised by every child who is lost in reverie watching a flower or wishing with all her heart on a birthday candle. In Eastern religions, meditation is seen as the pathway inwards from the noise and demands of the world to stillness and many of the icons of the Hindu deities, especially the Mother Goddesses, are depicted in the lotus position. In Ayurvedic holistic medicine, periods of meditation are built into every day, in the morning and late afternoon or early evening.

Meditating on your Tarot cards not only helps you to attain deeper levels of understanding of the images that enrich your readings, but extends your psychic awareness.

Tarot meditation

Meditation may seem a million light years from your own frantic world right now for some of us and yet if you have ever sat by a fountain and let your imagination merge with the running water or gazed into a candle flame and let all thoughts slip from you, you have been in a spontaneous state of meditation or altered consciousness. Women who do meditate, even for a few minutes each day or two or three times a week, benefit not only physically from their lowered blood pressure and heart rate, but also from their increased sense of well-being and the ability to cope with life in a calmer, more positive way. The early morning or evening are especially good times, or before bed to slow down the day and ensure positive dreams and quiet sleep. If you have not carried out any structured psychic development work previously, meditation is an excellent way of letting go of the conscious thoughts and strictures that can block the flow of unconscious symbolism that opens the door to other dimensions and to the wisdom deep within our psyche.

Preparing for meditation

- ✪ Sit either in the light of a large purple candle scented with lavender or in a pool of sunlight with a pot of scented flowers or herbs close to you.

- ✪ If you have a small water feature or bubbling fish tank, use that for background sound or play gentle music of the sea, the calling of dolphins or birdsong. Psychic awareness is a multi-sensory experience and by stimulating the senses initially you will find that during your meditative states colours seem brighter, sounds purer and fragrances more intense.

- ✪ Select a card from the Major Arcana that has vibrant colours – the Morgan Greer pack are, I find, especially good for psychic work. However, the Devil, Death and Tower, while having very positive divinatory meanings, are less suitable for meditative techniques as they may contain issues that should be resolved over a period of time in divination.

Beginning meditation

Meditation requires you to do nothing, merely open yourself to the impressions emanating from your card so that all others recede.

- ✪ Prop your card so that it is easily visible from where you are sitting. Some people photocopy or scan a card into a computer and enlarge the image two or three times. There are also large-sized packs, especially some of the reproduction mediaeval Tarot that are jewel-like in brilliance, but quite difficult to shuffle and so not popular in divination. You may also find a picture frame of the right size that you can slip the different Tarot images into. The Internet offers a number of sites from which you can download card images for non-commercial purposes.

Relaxing

Some people, myself included, find it hard to relax the different parts of their body when asked to do so as a prelude to meditation, or 'past life' work. In fact, I am guaranteed to tense every muscle, especially in the presence of a particularly ethereal New Age guru. This method is one I was taught many years ago before my first TV show in the US when I was so scared I could not stop shaking and that I have subsequently used many times. However, you may have your own method that already works for you.

✪ Sit in a chair, with both feet flat on the floor; if you wish, support your back with a pillow and have armrests on the chair for your elbows. You must be comfortable or it will be hard to meditate.

✪ In the sitting position, rest your arms comfortably in your lap with palms upwards. Some people prefer to sit cross-legged on the floor with their hands supporting their knees.

✪ Beginning either at your head or feet, tense and relax each part in turn. Use the following visualisation exercise to help you.

✪ Feel your feet on warm soft sand and bury them as deeply as you can, pushing downwards and then releasing your toes to rest once more on the soft, smooth, sunny shore.

✪ See yourself enclosed in a rainbow bubble. Push upwards with your arms as high as they will go, so that they press against but do not penetrate the shimmering upper membrane, and then sink back.

✪ Push outwards now to touch the bubble on either side of you, so that again you feel the pliable indentation, then return your hands gently to your sides.

✪ Finally, visualise a beautiful butterfly hovering over your head. Hold your neck and shoulders, your chest and finally your abdomen motionless as the butterfly lands on each of them in turn and relax each part as the butterfly flutters downwards and away.

Entering the light

☸ Do not begin with a specific question, but as your body slows down, let your mind gradually empty by visualising your thoughts as water pouring from a crystal jug into a stream and flowing away down a hillside, or stars in a brilliant sky disappearing one by one until there is inky blackness.

☸ When you feel totally relaxed, focus on a single circle or sphere of golden light or rich colour within the chosen card, for example the Sun or the globe of the world on the Empress's sceptre or the stars in her crown. Concentrate on breathing, slowly and deeply.

☸ Breathe in through your nose, hold it for a slow count of 'one and two and three' and slowly exhale through your mouth.

☸ As you inhale and exhale again, visualise the golden or coloured light from the card entering your body and dark light leaving with each released breath.

☸ Become your breathing, while remaining focused on the picture.

☸ Continue, and with each in-breath gradually visualise the Tarot image drawing around you so that you are within the card, bathed in its colours.

☸ Do not consciously attempt to move beyond the scene. However, you may find you do spontaneously experience visions of the past or pass through a doorway within the card to other realms. If so, accept this as a sign that you have tuned rapidly into your innate psychic abilities.

☸ Let the card world continue to expand and fill your mind, so that all other sights, sounds and sensations merge and the everyday world recedes even further.

☸ Allow any words and pictures also to come and go without attempting to hold or analyse them. Where Tarot meditation does differ from more general meditation techniques is that you may perceive, either externally or in your mind's vision, a clear image of one of the Tarot persona who at this particular point is of relevance to you.

❂ When you are ready, gradually move away from the focus, connecting with your breathing once more and letting the colours fade. As you do this, external sounds will return and your normal range of vision will expand until you are fully aware once more. Frequently the Tarot image will spontaneously begin to fade or the external world intrude and this is a sign that your mediation is complete. Duration may have little to do with the quality of your experience and the richest experiences can sometimes occur in a meditation of five minutes.

❂ Stretch your arms and legs again, like a cat waking after a long sleep, slowly and luxuriating in your relaxed state.

❂ Spend some time sitting in the candlelight, letting the Tarot world flow in and out of your consciousness. In the stillness, you may hear more words or see images in the candle flame. This time after meditation can be as rewarding as the experience itself.

❂ As you continue to work with your cards over the following weeks and months, you may spontaneously explore past life scenes either related to yourself or lives that seem connected with your own.

❂ You may hear messages channelled from your Tarot guardians and may find that a particular person, for example the High Priestess or the Hermit, will act as your guide, even if they are not featured in the specific card you are using.

Tarot visualisation

This is an empowering experience in which you do not simply allow experiences to happen as in meditation, but actively induce them. In practice, there is a great deal of overlap between the meditation and visualisation exercises.

❂ Select a card from the Major Arcana that has a doorway or obvious path from within the card.

✪ Begin with a gentle relaxation exercise (see page 175) and then initially use your imagination, the entrance to the psyche, to project yourself into and through your chosen card, for example on the path beyond the waterfall on the Empress card, into the forest, or across the cornfields. You may also enter the doorway of light behind the Hierophant's throne or dive deep into the pool of the Star maiden to where the world of the reflected cosmos and the lands below the sea may be found.

✪ As with meditation, breathe in slowly and draw the scene around you, breathing out very gently, gradually inhaling the colours, scents and sounds within the card.

✪ Visualise next a Tarot guide in the distance who gets nearer, perhaps a helpful Page, a kindly Queen, a Knight who will conduct you along at speed or even one of the Kings who may offer advice and an overview of life. Your Tarot guide may change according to your needs or remain the one you first meet in meditation. You can interact with your guide and, as you travel, you can explore different avenues that may shed light on your worldly or spiritual life path.

✪ When you are ready, move back to your entrance point, thank your guide and let the colours, sounds and fragrances fade.

In time you will find that you are no longer consciously creating the initial part of the experience – at this point your psyche is taking over. You can use Tarot exploration for past life work, for exploring other worlds or even the future, and as your psychic powers evolve, so will your readings become richer and more focused, using the Tarot cards as your entrance. Some Minor Arcana cards also provide a suitable focus for visualisation work.

Tarot magic

When you empowered your cards and created a circle of protection, you were using Tarot for magic. The advantage of Tarot rituals is that the cards contain all the symbols and ritual tools you need for spells and all you require in addition is a few candles and other basic artefacts you already have around your home.

Tarot spells

First you need to create a magical area for working: this can be the table on which you carry out your readings or a special circular table.

✪ Place a dark cloth on the table and stand two white pillar candles on it, the one to the left hand for the god or the male, animus energies, and the one on the right for the goddess, female or anima energies.

✪ Use a cylindrical crystal to draw an invisible, unbroken circle clockwise in the air or visualise a circle of light beginning from the north of the circle; if the table is round, the unseen line can follow the line of the table. You can use a compass to identify magnetic north, but this is not necessary if you are familiar with the geography of your area and know in which direction you would find north.

✪ Light your goddess and then your god candle.

✪ Place your four Aces in the four main compass positions, beginning with the Ace of Pentacles in the north, then the Ace of Swords in the east, the Ace of Wands in the south and finally the Ace of Cups in the west.

✪ Next, light in order four small candles, one to stand behind each card, green for Pentacles, yellow for Swords, red for Wands and blue for Cups.

(Some traditions begin in the east, the direction of the rising sun, but most traditional forms of magic use the north as the source of power, as I have suggested.)

✪ Next, you need a focus card for your ritual and that can be as varied as your imagination. For example, the Ten or King of Pentacles might be a good focus for attracting money and you could then surround it with coins or jewellery to add to the wealth-creating energies. The Lovers would be the obvious choice for a relationship issue, encircled by flowers. The Eight of Wands could be for travel, perhaps placed on a postcard of the place you wished to visit and the Eight of Pentacles for a career change or for learning a new skill, set on top of a job advertisement or under a silver charm to indicate a trade.

❂ Having set up your circle and focus, you need to raise the power, either by words, actions or both, to endow your focus card with energies which you will then release into the cosmos to set the power flowing. Each element has its own substance and these can be set next to the appropriate Ace.

❂ In the north, place a small dish of salt for Earth and in the east incense for Air, for example frankincense or myrrh, which are used in ceremonies. Next, place a gold candle for Fire in the south; in the west, for Water, set a dish of water in which rose petals have been soaked or pure spring water left open to the sun and the moonlight for 24 hours.

❂ First, summon your Guardian of the Northern Watchtower, by taking the salt and holding it over the Ace of Pentacles, saying

Guardian of the North, aid my endeavour.

❂ Then sprinkle a circle of salt around your focal card in the centre of the table, saying:

Guardian of the North, Mistress of the Ancient Stones,
bring this my wish to fruition.

❂ Return the salt to its place, and light next the incense, calling on the Guardian of the Eastern Watchtower as you hold the incense above the Ace of Swords:

Guardian of the East, aid my endeavour.

❂ Next, circle the incense nine times around your focal card, saying:

Guardian of the East, Master of the mighty Winds,
bring this my wish to fruition.

❂ Return the incense to the east and leave it burning.

❂ Light the golden candle and taking care not to drip wax on the card (a broad-based holder will prevent this), hold it high above the Ace of Wands, saying:

Guardian of the Southern Watchtower, aid my endeavour.

☻ Circle now the central focus card nine times with the candle, saying:

> Guardian of the South, Master of the Lightning Flare,
> bring this my wish to fruition.

☻ Return the candle to the south and leave it to burn.

☻ Finally, take the dish of water and, holding it above the Ace of Cups, say:

> Guardian of the Western Watchtower, aid my endeavour.

☻ Sprinkle nine drops of water over the salt circle surrounding the central card, saying:

> Guardian of the West and Mistress of the tumultuous oceans,
> bring this my wish to fruition.

☻ Return the water to the west.

Now you need to raise the power. The easiest way is by a chant that increases in intensity and speed.

☻ Holding the focal card between your hands in the centre of the circle, visualise a cone of brilliant rainbow light, building up around the cards; the cone gets larger and higher as you chant, and begins to swirl as though it were within a vortex. You can now link the chant to the purpose of the spell: for example, if you wanted money, you could hold the King of Pentacles and visualise the pile of coins rising higher and higher, empowered by the cone of power, as you chant:

> Cone of Power, bring wealth this Hour.

☻ Raise the card higher and higher until it is above your head, but still in the centre of the circle and see the cone enclosing you within its spiralling brilliance, adding energy to your words.

☻ When you feel as though you can contain the power no longer, with a final cry,

> The wish is mine!

bring the card down in a slashing movement, away from your body so that it ends up at waist level, within the circle.

- Visualise the energies spiralling into the cosmos like a huge rainbow firework as the cone explodes and falls as a golden star – or, in a money spell, as a shower of golden coins.

- Blow out your elemental candles in the reverse order of lighting, thanking your guardians for their protection and finally snuff or blow out the goddess and then the god candle.

- Uncast the circle, either visualising the light fading or moving your crystal around the invisible line, this time in an anti-clockwise direction from the north.

- Dispose of the used materials in an environmentally-friendly way and sleep with the focus card, surrounded by the four Aces and any other symbols, such as coins or flowers, by your bed.

A Tarot love ritual

Susan, who is in her early fifties and divorced, has met Gary, a divorcee of the same age, who comes every week into the office she manages, to check the computers. They get on well and have been for meals several times but she is afraid of rejection if she tells Gary she would like more than friendship and Gary is very shy and is unlikely to make the first move.

She does not want to carry out a formal ritual, but uses the correspondences with the cards and adapts the basic ideas.

- Susan took the Lovers card, plus the King of Cups to represent Gary and the Queen of Wands for herself.

- She placed the Lovers card in the centre, his card to the left and her own to the right and lit two identical green candles, the colour of Venus and love, the first, Gary's, behind the King of Cups and her own behind the Queen of Wands. She circled the three cards and candles with pink glass nuggets arranged touching each other, to make a magical circle (pink is another colour associated with Venus), saying:

So do I encircle my love that over the coming weeks we may grow closer.

❂ When the circle was complete, Susan moved the two Court Cards and candles nearer to each other, saying:

So do we each move nearer the other's heart.

❂ She blew out the candles in the reverse order to lighting, sending the love to Gary and left the three cards and the circle of nuggets on the table.

❂ At the same time the next evening, she lit first her own candle, then his, and surrounded the Lovers card with forget-me-nots:

So do I bring my love this token of my fidelity. May he feel the same.

❂ She lit next rose incense, a flower associated with love and Venus and circled the three cards and candles with the incense stick nine times saying:

Fragrance of love, stars above, Gary move, to love me.

❂ Susan moved the candles and Court Cards even closer so that the Court Cards were touching the Lovers, saying:

As we move nearer in spirit, so may we meet on the earthly plane in harmony.

❂ Then she blew out the candles, in reverse order of lighting, sending the love to Gary and left the candles, flowers, cards and circle of nuggets.

❂ On the third evening at the same time, she took an oil burner and heated ylang-ylang, an oil of love and passion. She lit the candles, first his and then her own, and passed first his card and then her own card nine times over the oil, saying:

Love, grow, love show Gary I care.
Love shine, be mine, life to share.

❂ She then placed the two Court Cards facing each other on top of the Lovers card and moved the candles so that they were touching, saying:

Meet in love.

⊗ On this final night of the ritual, Susan left the candles to burn
down before removing the cards and placing them under her
pillow; she left the flowers circled by the nuggets next to her
bed.

The next morning was Saturday and to Susan's amazement she
received a phone call from an embarrassed and slightly
bewildered Gary to say he had two tickets for a play she wanted to
see. He stuttered that his sister had had to cancel at the last
minute. Coincidence? Telepathy? Was Gary also looking for an
opportunity to further their relationship? Or had Susan's Tarot
spell worked? At the very least it gave her the confidence to reveal
her deepening feelings and six months later they were flat-
hunting together.

Susan used her own words and adapted the basic template to suit
her needs. The best magic is that created for a specific need,
prompted by positive intent and not bound by rules. Susan said
she just knew what to do. If we listen to our inner voice we are all
natural magicians as well as Tarot readers, for the knowledge of
our wise ancestors is buried in our genes.

DAY 30
Where next?

✛

Once you can use the Tarot, you may go on to study it in depth. But though you may read books and attend courses, the best source of wisdom will always be your own unconscious mind that can tap the Tribal Voice of other women in other times and places, who loved and worried and laughed and cried down the millennia – and you speak with that same Voice. As you evolve spiritually, so the cards will become more of an extension of your psyche and enable you to explore past, present and future, without consciously applying Tarot meanings or analysing the positions of the cards. And one day you will give a brilliant reading and realise afterwards you did not look at the cards even once – and that is incredibly scary, but very exciting.

You may continue to read only for yourself, friends and acquaintances, or perhaps when you feel confident you may give Tarot readings to strangers – there will be no shortage of people in the office, at parties and friends of friends of friends who will be eager to come to you for a consultation. But remember they bring to you their hearts and hopes and fears and so you will find yourself crying and laughing and sharing the secrets they would not tell their mother, best friend or doctor. I once had a man come to me in a crowded London bookshop and I could make no sense of his reading. He told me then he had just learned he was dying and I had a kind face.

If you do turn professional, you should charge for your time just as any other consultant would do – and you may be asked to deliver miracles by solving marital, career and even sexual problems. The temptation is to give good news even if there is none. Instead, try to identify small positive ways in which the questioner can find a little happiness each day, even if her cards reveal no immediately fruitful potential avenues. Because for every person who comes to you for a reading about their spiritual path, there will be ten with cheating husbands, difficult families, money and health worries.

Tarot reading can be the most rewarding job in the world, but it is incredibly exhausting. But whether you become a Tarot expert on a top television programme or a woman who uses the Tarot late in the evening to explore her own spirituality or simply to say 'I exist', the magic resides, not in the cards, but in *you*. You are special, so love and believe in yourself and a year from now you will be amazed at how far you have travelled – and how far ahead you can now see.

Further reading

✛

The Tarot
Richard Cavendish, *The Tarot*, Chancellor Press, 1988

Eileen Connolly, *A New Handbook for the Apprentice*, Aquarian, 1995

Cassandra Eason, *The Complete Book of the Tarot*, Piatkus, 1999

Jean Freer, *The New Feminist Tarot*, Aquarian, 1987

Cynthia Giles, *Tarot, the Complete Guide*, Robert Hale, 1993

Stuart Kaplan, *The Encyclopaedia of Tarot*, US Games System, 1990

Gareth Knight, *The Magical World of the Tarot*, Aquarian, 1992

Jane Lyle, *The Renaissance Tarot* (cards and book), Piatkus, 1998

Kathleen McCormack, *An Historical Guide to the Tarot*, Aurum Press, 1998

Sally Nichols, *Jung and Tarot, an Archetypal Journey*, Samuel Weiser, New York

Carl Sargent, *Personality, Divination and the Tarot*, Destiny Books, 1988

A E Waite, *The Key to the Tarot*, Rider Books, 1986

Candle magic
Ray Buckland, *Advanced Candle Magic*, Llewellyn, St Paul, Minnesota, 1996

Cassandra Eason, *Candle Power*, Blandford, 1999

Chakras
Karagulla Shafica and Van Gelder Kunz Dora, *Chakras and the Human Energy Field*, Theosophical University Press, 1994

Naomi Ozaniec, *The Elements of the Chakras*, Element, 1989

Incenses and oils

Scott Cunningham, *Complete Book of Oils, Incenses and Brews*, Llewellyn, St Paul, Minnesota, 1991

Gerena Dunwich, *Wicca Garden: A Witch's Guide to Magical and Enchanted Herbs and Plants*, Citadel, Carol, New York, 1996

Magic

Cassandra Eason, *The Complete Book of Magic and Ritual*, Piatkus, 1999

Cassandra Eason, *Every Woman A Witch*, Quantum, 1996

Silver Ravenwolf, *To Ride a Silver Broomstick: New Generation Witchcraft*, Llewellyn, St Paul, Minnesota, 1995

Meditation and visualisation

Barbara Brown, *New Mind, New Body*, Bantam, 1975

Helen Graham, *Visualisation, an Introductory Guide*, Piatkus, 1996

Lawrence LeShan, *How to Meditate*, Crucible, 1989

Shamanism

Carlos Casteneda, *Journey to Ixtlan*, Penguin, 1972

Piers Vittebsky, *The Shaman*, Macmillan, 1995

Roger N Walsh, *The Spirit of Shamanism*, Jeremy P Tarcher, Los Angeles, 1990

Index